WHAT'S COOKING

Soups

Carole Clements

THUNDER BAY
P·R·E·S·S

First published in the United States in 2000 by
Thunder Bay Press
An imprint of the Advantage Publishers Group
5880 Oberlin Drive, San Diego, CA 92121-4794
www.advantagebooksonline.com

A Parragon book, Parragon, Queen Street House, 4 Queen Street, Bath BA1 1HE, UK

Library of Congress Cataloging in Publication Data

What's cooking : soups.
        p. cm.
    Includes index.
    ISBN 1-57145-250-8
    1. Soups.
TX757.W44 2000
641.8 13--dc21   00-020510

Printed in China
3 4 01 02 03
Produced by Haldane Mason, London

Acknowledgments
Editorial Consultant: Felicity Jackson
Photography: Colin Bowling, Paul Forrester, and Stephen Brayne
Home Economists and Stylist: David Morgan, Mandy Phipps, Gina Steer
All props supplied by Barbara Stewart at Surfaces.

NOTE

Unless otherwise stated, milk is assumed to be full fat,
eggs are medium, and pepper is freshly ground black pepper.

Recipes using uncooked eggs should be
avoided by infants, the elderly, pregnat women, and anyone
suffering from an illness

Contents

Introduction

Soup is one of the most fundamental forms of food. Its traditions go back to the earliest days of civilized man with the advent of fire. It remains a favorite source of nourishment and pleasure today and homemade soup has become a special treat.

The benefits of soup are numerous. It is nutritious, satisfying to eat, and generally lean. It is economical to make, especially using abundant seasonal produce, but even expensive ingredients like lobster go further when made into soups.

Making soup can be a very creative endeavor, as satisfying for the cook as the recipients. Practice hones skills and promotes confidence. This book offers an array of different styles of soup, using a variety of ingredients and techniques. Consider the recipes as a framework of proportions, and experiment with alternative ingredients if you wish.

EQUIPMENT

Soup-making requires little in the way of basic equipment. A good knife or two and a large saucepan with a lid are essential. A stock pot, or a large capacity cast-iron casserole, is also useful. Other things needed to expedite your efforts are probably already in your kitchen— a cutting board, colander, sieves, vegetable peeler, scissors, ladle, spoons. A fat separator or degreasing pitcher is helpful, as is a large capacity measuring cup.

A wide range of specialized equipment is available, but not necessarily essential for making soups. For puréeing soups, the various options produce differing results. A food mill, the most economical choice, will do the basic job of producing relatively smooth soups and it also sieves at the same time. For the smoothest and best texture, nothing beats a blender. A food processor may be used for chopping and slicing ingredients as well as puréeing cooked soups, so it performs a variety of functions. A hand-held blender can purée right in the saucepan, as long as the depth of liquid is appropriate.

These pieces of equipment may each have a role to play in soup-making, but it's best to experiment first and see what you really need for the soups you like to make before investing. For most people, there is no need for a horde of equipment. Always follow manufacturer's instructions and recommendations for safe operation of electric appliances.

INGREDIENTS

Soups are as good as the ingredients in them. While leftovers have traditionally been a springboard for creativity in soup-making, and may certainly provide useful components, fresh ingredients at their peak provide optimum nutritional benefits and taste.

Water is the most basic ingredient for soup. Even stock is essentially flavored water. Many soups taste best made with water, as the pure flavors are highlighted, this is especially true of vegetable soups.

Some soups make their own stock during the cooking process. Others call for stock as an ingredient. This can be homemade, bought ready-made, made up from stock cubes, powder or liquid stock base, or canned consommé or clear broth. It is useful to know how to make stock, as homemade is more economical and normally has superior flavor.

STOCK-MAKING

Making stock is easy. After getting it underway, it requires little attention, just time. You can save stock ingredients in the freezer until you need them: chicken carcasses, giblets, necks, backs, and trimmings; scraps and bones from meat roasts;

vegetable trimmings such as leek greens, celery leaves and stems, mushroom stalks, pieces of carrot, and unused onion halves.

Recipes appear throughout the book for Fish Stock (see page 102), Beef Stock (see page 108), Chicken Stock (see page 128), and meat stock (see page 228). The following general points cover the basic techniques of stock-making.

Fresh ingredients are determined by the kind of stock you want. Chicken or turkey wings are inexpensive and provide excellent flavor for poultry stock. Veal bones give more flavor than beef and pork bones lend sweetness. Lamb or ham bones are not suitable for a general purpose meat stock, as the flavors are too pronounced, but can make delicious stocks when their flavors are appropriate, such as ham stock for split pea or bean soup.

Aromatic vegetables—carrot, onion, leek, garlic, for instance—are almost always included in stock. Strongly flavored vegetables like cabbage or rutabaga should be used sparingly, as the stock produced would be unsuitable for delicate soups. Avoid dark greens as they make stock murky.

Except when a pale, delicate stock is desired, browning the main ingredients first, either by roasting or frying, adds color and richer flavor to the stock. Adding a roast chicken carcass or two is an easy way to do this.

Use cold water to make stock; it helps extract impurities. For a flavorful stock, keep the amount of water in proportion to the ingredients, which should be covered by about 2 inches. Skim off the foam that rises to the surface as stock is heated, as it contains impurities that can make stock cloudy. Cook stock uncovered and do not allow it to boil at any point or fat may be incorporated into the liquid, unable to be removed.

Stock needs slow cooking over a low heat. Beef or meat stock takes 4–6 hours to extract maximum flavor, chicken or other poultry stock 2–3 hours. Fish stock only requires about half an hour of cooking.

Remove the fat from stock before using. The easiest way to do this is to refrigerate it, allowing the fat to congeal, then lift off the fat. If time is short, use a fat separator (a jug or pitcher with the spout at the bottom) to remove the fat from warm stock, or spoon off the fat, although that is not nearly as effective as the other methods.

For greater flavor, stock can be reduced—cooked slowly, uncovered, to reduce and concentrate it. This procedure may also be useful to reduce the volume for storage. Stock keeps refrigerated for about 3 days or frozen for several months.

SERVING SOUP

Soup is more flexible in terms of portions than many other foods. In this book a range of servings may be indicated, as a soup will provide more servings as a starter than as the focus of a meal. Starter portions range from 1 cup for a very rich soup to 1½ cups; main course portions from 1⅔ cups to about 2½ cups.

Soup is a perfect food for almost any occasion, from the most casual to the very formal. It can set the tone for the rest of a meal or be the meal itself. It brings satisfaction to those who make it as well as those who eat it and nourishes both the body and the soul.

Vegetable Soups

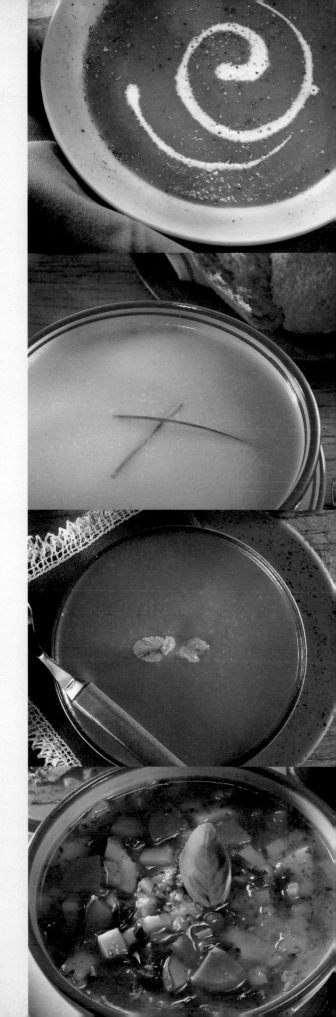

Vegetables offer an enormous range of options for making soups. Often the simplest soups to make, they also provide the most versatility. Think of each vegetable as the growing season unfolds and the innumerable ways each can be used in soups—creamy soups, broths, chunky soups, thick and hearty soups. Vegetables provide simple nourishment or dramatic complexity, pure flavors or fascinating amalgamations, lean and healthy alliances or rich, tempting combinations.

Vegetable soups are endlessly variable and eminently enjoyable—and often beautifully colored, as well. They can provide a light starter to introduce a meal or a hearty and satisfying main course. While most soups are suitable for preparing ahead, vegetable soups are usually quickly cooked and often keep longer than other soups.

Remember, the best ingredients make the best soups. Plump, fresh vegetables provide more flavor and nutrition than tired, wrinkly ones and soups should never be a repository for vegetables that are seriously past their prime. Use plenty of vegetables. A high proportion of vegetables to liquid promotes concentrated flavors, as well as a pleasing density.

Which vegetables to use for soup is a personal choice. The recipes that follow offer many ideas. Consider them a platform for experimentation.

Fresh Mushroom Soup

When you see mushrooms at a special price in your local supermarket, think of this soup.
Porcini, portobello, or chanterelle mushrooms are especially tasty.

Serves 4

INGREDIENTS

3 tbsp. butter
1 lb. 9 oz. mushrooms, sliced
1 onion, finely chopped
1 shallot, finely chopped
3 tbsp. all-purpose flour

2–3 tbsp. dry white wine or sherry
6 cups chicken or vegetable stock
²/₃ cup light cream
2 tbsp. chopped fresh parsley
fresh lemon juice (optional)

salt and pepper
4 tbsp. sour cream or crème fraîche,
  to garnish

1 Melt half the butter in a large frying pan over a medium heat. Add the mushrooms and season with salt and pepper. Cook for about 8 minutes until they are golden brown, stirring occasionally at first, then more often after they start to color. Remove the mushrooms from the heat.

2 Melt the remaining butter in a saucepan over a medium heat, add the onion and shallot and cook for 2–3 minutes until just softened. Stir the flour into the pan and continue cooking for 2 minutes. Add the wine and stock and stir well.

3 Set aside about one quarter of the mushrooms. Add the remainder to the pan. Reduce the heat, cover and cook gently for 20 minutes, stirring occasionally.

4 Allow the soup to cool slightly, then transfer to a blender or food processor and purée until smooth, working in batches, if necessary. (If using a food processor, strain off the cooking liquid and reserve. Purée the soup solids with enough cooking liquid to moisten them, then combine with the remaining liquid.)

5 Return the soup to the saucepan and stir in the reserved mushrooms, the cream and parsley. Cook for about 5 minutes to heat through. Taste and adjust the seasoning, adding a few drops of lemon juice if wished. Ladle into warm bowls and decorate with sour cream.

Fresh Tomato Soup

Made with fresh tomatoes, the taste of this soup is subtle and complex.
Basil is a proven partner for tomatoes, but you could also try tarragon.

Serves 4

INGREDIENTS

1 kg/2 lb. 4 oz. ripe plum tomatoes, skinned
2 tsp. olive oil
1 large sweet onion, finely chopped
1 carrot, finely chopped

1 stalk celery, finely chopped
2 garlic cloves, finely chopped or crushed
1 tsp. fresh marjoram leaves, or ¼ tsp. dried marjoram

2 cups water
4–5 tbsp. heavy cream, plus extra to garnish
2 tbsp. chopped fresh basil leaves
salt and pepper

1 Cut the tomatoes in half and scrape the seeds into a sieve set over a bowl to catch the juice. Reserve the juice and discard the seeds. Chop the tomato flesh into large chunks.

2 Heat the olive oil in a large saucepan. Add the onion, carrot and celery and cook over a medium-low heat for 3–4 minutes, stirring occasionally.

3 Add the tomatoes and their juice, with the garlic and marjoram. Cook for 2 minutes.

Stir in the water, reduce the heat and simmer, covered, for about 45 minutes until the vegetables are very soft, stirring occasionally.

4 Allow the soup to cool slightly, then transfer to a blender or food processor and purée until smooth, working in batches, if necessary. (If using a food processor, strain off the cooking liquid and reserve. Purée the soup solids with enough cooking liquid to moisten them, then combine with the remaining liquid.)

5 Return the soup to the saucepan and place over a medium-low heat. Add the cream and stir in the basil. Season with salt and pepper and heat through; do not allow to boil.

6 Ladle the soup into warm bowls and swirl a little extra cream into each serving. Serve at once.

COOK'S TIP

For the best flavor, this soup needs to be made with ripe tomatoes. If supermarket tomatoes are pale and hard, leave them to ripen at room temperature for several days. This is especially important in winter when most tomatoes are picked and shipped before they are ripe.

Cheese & Vegetable Chowder

For this soup, the root vegetables should be cut into small dice so that they all cook in the same amount of time. Dicing the vegetables also gives the soup an attractive look.

Serves 4

INGREDIENTS

2 tbsp. butter
1 large onion, finely chopped
1 large leek, split lengthwise and
   thinly sliced
1–2 garlic cloves, crushed
6 tbsp. all-purpose flour
5 cups chicken or vegetable stock

3 carrots, finely diced
2 stalks celery, finely diced
1 turnip, finely diced
1 large potato, finely diced
3–4 sprigs fresh thyme, or ⅛ tsp.
   dried thyme
1 bay leaf

1½ cups light cream
10½ oz. mature Cheddar cheese,
   grated
2 tbsp. chopped mixed fresh parsley,
   tarragon and chives
fresh chopped parsley, to garnish
salt and pepper

1 Melt the butter in a large heavy-based saucepan over a medium-low heat. Add the onion, leek and garlic. Cover and cook for about 5 minutes, stirring frequently, until the vegetables start to soften.

2 Stir the flour into the vegetables and continue cooking for 2 minutes. Add a little of the stock and stir well, scraping the bottom of the pan to mix in the flour. Bring to a boil, stirring frequently, and slowly stir in the rest of the stock.

3 Add the carrots, celery, turnip, potato, thyme, and bay leaf. Reduce the heat, cover and cook gently for about 35 minutes, stirring occasionally, until the vegetables are tender. Remove the bay leaf and the thyme branches.

4 Stir in the cream and simmer over a very low heat for 5 minutes. Add the cheese a handful at a time, stirring constantly for 1 minute after each addition, to make sure it is completely melted. Taste the soup and adjust the seasoning, adding salt if needed, and pepper to taste. Ladle immediately into warm bowls, sprinkle with fresh chopped parsley and serve.

Spinach Soup

This soup has a rich brilliant color and an intense pure flavor. You can taste the goodness!
Ready-washed spinach makes it especially quick to make.

Serves 4

INGREDIENTS

1 tbsp. olive oil
1 onion, halved and thinly sliced
1 leek, split lengthwise and thinly
    sliced
1 potato, finely diced

4 cups water
2 sprigs fresh marjoram or ¼ tsp.
    dried
2 sprigs fresh thyme or ¼ tsp. dried
1 bay leaf

14 oz. young spinach, washed
freshly grated nutmeg
salt and pepper
4 tbsp. light cream, to serve

1 Heat the oil in a heavy-based saucepan over a medium heat. Add the onion and leek and cook for about 3 minutes, stirring occasionally, until they begin to soften.

2 Add the potato, water, marjoram, thyme, and bay leaf, along with a large pinch of salt. Bring to a boil, reduce the heat, cover and cook gently for about 25 minutes until the vegetables are tender. Remove the bay leaf and the herb stems.

3 Add the spinach and continue cooking for 3–4 minutes, stirring frequently, just until it is completely wilted.

4 Allow the soup to cool slightly, then transfer to a blender or food processor and purée until smooth, working in batches if necessary. (If using a food processor, strain off the cooking liquid and reserve. Purée the soup solids with enough cooking liquid to moisten them, then combine with the remaining liquid.)

5 Return the soup to the saucepan and thin with a little more water, if wished. Season with salt, a good grinding of pepper and a generous grating of nutmeg. Place over a low heat and simmer until reheated.

6 Ladle the soup into warm bowls and swirl a tablespoonful of cream into each serving.

Roasted Pumpkin & Tomato Soup

This soup is a wonderful way to use autumn harvest vegetables. Make it when tomatoes are still plentiful and pumpkins are appearing in local farmers' markets.

Serves 4

INGREDIENTS

1–2 tbsp. olive oil

2 lb. peeled pumpkin flesh, cut into slices ¾ inch thick

1 lb. ripe tomatoes, skinned, cored and thickly sliced

1 onion, chopped

2 garlic cloves, finely chopped

4 tbsp. white wine

2 tbsp. water

2½ cups chicken or vegetable stock

½ cup light cream

salt and pepper

snipped chives, to garnish

1 Drizzle 1 tablespoon of the olive oil over the base of a large baking dish. Layer the pumpkin, tomatoes, onion and garlic in 2 or 3 layers. Drizzle the top with the remaining olive oil, pour over the wine and water. Season with a little salt and pepper.

2 Cover with kitchen foil and bake in a preheated oven at 375° F for about 45 minutes, or until all the vegetables are soft.

3 Allow the vegetables to cool slightly, then transfer to a blender or food processor and add the cooking juices and as much stock as needed to cover the vegetables. Purée until smooth, working in batches if necessary.

4 Pour the purée into a saucepan and stir in the remaining stock. Cook gently over a medium heat, stirring occasionally, for about 15 minutes, or until heated through. Stir in the cream and continue cooking for 3–4 minutes.

5 Taste and adjust the seasoning, if necessary. Ladle the soup into warm bowls, garnish with chives and serve.

VARIATIONS

Serve the soup with crispy garlic croutons, if you wish, instead of chives. You could substitute butternut or acorn squash for the pumpkin.

Eggplant Soup

The parsnip and carrot bring a balancing sweetness to the eggplant in this delicious soup.

Serves 6

INGREDIENTS

1 tbsp. olive oil, plus extra for
  brushing
1½ lb. eggplant, halved lengthwise
1 carrot, halved
1 small parsnip, halved
2 onions, finely chopped
3 garlic cloves, finely chopped

4 cups chicken or vegetable stock
¼ tsp. fresh thyme leaves, or a pinch
  of dried thyme
1 bay leaf
⅛ tsp. ground coriander
1 tbsp. tomato paste
⅔ cup light cream

freshly squeezed lemon juice
salt and pepper

LEMON-GARLIC SEASONING:
grated rind of ½ lemon
1 garlic clove, finely chopped
3 tbsp. chopped fresh parsley

1 Oil a shallow roasting pan and add the eggplant, cut sides down, and the carrot and parsnip. Brush the vegetables with oil. Roast in a preheated oven at 400° F for 30 minutes, turning once.

2 When cool enough to handle, scrape the eggplant flesh away from the skin, or

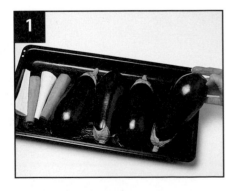

scoop it out, then roughly chop. Cut the parsnip and carrot into chunks.

3 Heat the oil in a large saucepan over a medium-low heat. Add the onions and garlic and cook for about 5 minutes, stirring frequently, until softened. Add the eggplant, parsnip, carrot, stock, thyme, bay leaf, coriander, and tomato paste, with a little salt. Stir to combine. Cover and simmer for 30 minutes, or until very tender.

4 Allow the soup to cool slightly, then transfer to a blender or food processor and purée until smooth, working in batches if necessary. (If using a

food processor, strain off the cooking liquid and reserve. Purée the soup solids with enough cooking liquid to moisten them, then combine with the remaining liquid.)

5 Return the puréed soup to the saucepan and stir in the cream. Reheat the soup over a low heat for about 10 minutes until hot. Adjust the seasoning, adding lemon juice to taste.

6 To make the lemon-garlic seasoning, chop together the lemon rind, garlic, and parsley until very fine and well mixed. Ladle the soup into warm bowls, then garnish with some freshly chopped parsley.

Cauliflower & Cider Soup

This soup was inspired by a visit to Normandy where cider and cream are plentiful, and are combined in many local specialities.

Serves 4

INGREDIENTS

2 tbsp. butter
1 onion, finely chopped
1 garlic clove, crushed
1 carrot, thinly sliced
1¼ lb. cauliflower florets (from 1

medium head)
2½ cups hard cider
freshly grated nutmeg
½ cup milk
½ cup heavy cream

salt and pepper
snipped chives, to garnish

1 Melt the butter in a saucepan over a medium heat. Add the onion and garlic and cook for about 5 minutes, stirring occasionally, until just softened.

2 Add the carrot and cauliflower to the pan and pour over the cider. Season with salt, pepper, and a generous grating of nutmeg. Bring to a boil, then reduce the heat to low. Cover and cook gently for about 50 minutes until the vegetables are very soft.

3 Allow the soup to cool slightly, then transfer to a blender or food processor and purée until smooth, working in batches if necessary. (If using a food processor, strain off the cooking liquid and reserve. Purée the soup solids with enough cooking liquid to moisten them, then combine with the remaining liquid.)

4 Return the soup to the saucepan and stir in the milk and cream. Taste and adjust the seasoning, if necessary. Simmer the soup over a low heat, stirring occasionally, until heated through.

5 Ladle the soup into warm bowls, garnish with chives, and serve.

COOK'S TIP

If you don't have hard cider, substitute ½ cup each white wine, apple juice, and water.

Broccoli Soup with Cream Cheese

This soup highlights the rich flavor of broccoli. It is a popular vegetable with almost everyone and particularly healthy. If you prefer a smooth soup, purée it before serving.

Serves 4

INGREDIENTS

14 oz. broccoli (from 1 large head)
2 tsp. butter
1 tsp. oil
1 onion, finely chopped
1 leek, thinly sliced

1 small carrot, finely chopped
3 tbsp. white rice
3¾ cups water
1 bay leaf
4 tbsp. heavy cream

3½ oz. cream cheese
freshly grated nutmeg
salt and pepper
croutons, to serve (see Cook's Tip)

1 Divide the broccoli into small florets and cut off the stems. Peel the large stems and chop all the stems into small pieces.

2 Heat the butter and oil in a large saucepan over a medium heat and add the onion, leek and carrot. Cook for 3–4 minutes, stirring frequently, until the onion is soft.

3 Add the broccoli stems, rice, water, bay leaf, and a pinch of salt. Bring just to a boil and reduce the heat to low. Cover and simmer for 15 minutes. Add the broccoli florets and continue cooking, covered, for 15–20 minutes until the rice and vegetables are tender. Remove the bay leaf.

4 Stir in the cream and soft cheese. Season the soup with nutmeg, pepper and, if needed, more salt. Simmer over a low heat for a few minutes until heated through, stirring occasionally. Taste and adjust the seasoning, if needed. Ladle into warm bowls and serve sprinkled with croutons.

COOK'S TIP

To make croutons, remove the crusts from thick slices of bread, then cut the bread into dice. Fry in vegetable oil, stirring constantly, until evenly browned, then drain on paper towels.

Lettuce & Arugula Soup

Cooked lettuce tastes similar to sorrel, but lettuce is much easier to find and cheaper. Almost any kind of leafy lettuce will do, but iceberg does not have enough flavor.

Serves 4–6

INGREDIENTS

1 tbsp. butter
1 large sweet onion, halved and sliced
2 leeks, sliced
6¼ cups chicken stock
6 tbsp. white rice
2 carrots, thinly sliced

3 garlic cloves
1 bay leaf
2 heads soft round lettuce (about 1 lb. 2 oz), cored and chopped
¾ cup heavy cream
freshly grated nutmeg

3 oz. arugula leaves, finely chopped
salt and pepper

1 Heat the butter in a large saucepan over a medium heat and add the onion and leeks. Cover and cook for 3–4 minutes, stirring frequently, until the vegetables begin to soften.

2 Add the stock, rice, carrots, garlic, and bay leaf with a large pinch of salt. Bring just to a boil. Reduce the heat, cover and simmer for 25–30 minutes, or until the rice and vegetables are tender. Remove the bay leaf.

3 Add the lettuce and cook for 10 minutes, until the leaves are soft, stirring occasionally.

4 Allow the soup to cool slightly, then transfer to a blender or food processor and purée until smooth, working in batches if necessary. (If using a food processor, strain off the cooking liquid and reserve. Purée the soup solids with enough cooking liquid to moisten them, then combine with the remaining liquid.)

5 Return the soup to the saucepan and place over a medium-low heat. Stir in the cream and a grating of nutmeg. Simmer for about 5 minutes, stirring occasionally, until the soup is reheated. Add more water or cream if you prefer a thinner soup.

6 Add the arugula and simmer for 2–3 minutes, stirring occasionally, until it is wilted. Adjust the seasoning and ladle the soup into warm bowls.

Celery & Stilton Soup

This soup combines two ingredients that have been paired since Victorian times, when celery stalks were put in tall glass containers on the dining table, to eat with Stilton cheese.

Serves 4

INGREDIENTS

2 tbsp. butter
1 onion, finely chopped
4 large stalks celery, peeled and
   finely chopped

1 large carrot, finely chopped
4 cups chicken or vegetable stock
3–4 thyme sprigs
1 bay leaf

½ cup heavy cream
5 ½ oz. Stilton cheese, crumbled
freshly grated nutmeg
salt and pepper

1 Melt the butter in a large saucepan over a medium-low heat. Add the onion and cook for 3–4 minutes, stirring frequently, until just softened. Add the celery and carrot and continue cooking for 3 minutes. Season lightly with salt and pepper.

2 Add the stock, thyme, and bay leaf and bring to the boil. Reduce the heat, cover and simmer gently for about 25 minutes, stirring occasionally, until the vegetables are very tender.

3 Allow the soup to cool slightly and remove the bouquet garni. Transfer the soup to a blender or food processor and purée until smooth, working in batches, if necessary. (If using a food processor, strain off the cooking liquid and reserve. Purée the soup solids with enough cooking liquid to moisten them, then combine with the remaining liquid.)

4 Return the puréed soup to the saucepan and stir in the cream. Simmer over a low heat for 5 minutes.

5 Add the Stilton slowly, stirring constantly, until smooth. (Do not allow the soup to boil.) Taste and adjust the seasoning, adding salt, if needed, plenty of pepper, and nutmeg to taste.

6 Ladle into warm bowls, garnish with celery leaves and serve.

VARIATION

Substitute matured cheddar or Gruyère for the Stilton.

Jerusalem Artichoke & Rutabaga Soup

Select Jerusalem artichokes with few knobs, as there is less waste and they will be easier to peel.

Serves 4

INGREDIENTS

1 lb. 2 oz. Jerusalem artichokes

2 tsp. butter

1 onion, finely chopped

4 oz. peeled rutabaga, cubed

1 strip pared lemon rind

3 cups chicken or vegetable stock

3 tbsp. heavy cream

1 tbsp. fresh lemon juice, or to taste

4 tbsp. lightly toasted pine nuts

1 Peel the Jerusalem artichokes and cut large ones into pieces. Drop into a bowl of cold water to prevent discoloration.

2 Melt the butter in a large saucepan over a medium heat. Add the onion and cook for about 3 minutes, stirring frequently, until just softened.

3 Drain the Jerusalem artichokes and add them to the saucepan with the rutabaga and lemon rind. Pour in the stock, season with a little salt and pepper and stir to combine. Bring just to a boil, reduce the heat and simmer gently for about 20 minutes until the vegetables are tender.

4 Allow the soup to cool slightly, then transfer to a blender or food processor and purée until smooth. (If using a food processor, strain off the cooking liquid and reserve. Purée the soup solids with enough cooking liquid to moisten them, then combine with the remaining liquid.)

5 Return the soup to the saucepan, stir in the cream and simmer for about 5 minutes until reheated. Add the lemon juice. Taste and adjust the seasoning, adding more lemon juice if wished. Ladle the soup into warm bowls and very gently place the pine nuts on top, dividing them evenly. Serve at once.

Green Vegetable Soup with Basil Pesto

This soup takes advantage of summer vegetables bursting with flavor. If you find fresh flageolet beans, or other fresh beans, be sure to include them in place of the canned version.

Serves 6

INGREDIENTS

1 tbsp. olive oil
1 onion, finely chopped
1 large leek, split and thinly sliced
1 stalk celery, thinly sliced
1 carrot, quartered and thinly sliced
1 garlic clove, finely chopped
6 cups water
1 potato, diced
1 parsnip, finely diced
1 small kohlrabi or turnip, diced

5½ oz. green beans, cut in small pieces
5½ oz. fresh or frozen peas
2 small zucchini, quartered lengthwise and sliced
14 oz. can flageolet beans, drained and rinsed
3½ oz. spinach leaves, cut into thin ribbons
salt and pepper

PESTO:
1 large garlic clove, very finely chopped
½ oz. fresh basil leaves
2¾ oz. Parmesan cheese, grated
4 tbsp. extra-virgin olive oil

1 Heat the olive oil in a large saucepan over a medium-low heat. Add the onion and leek and cook for 5 minutes, stirring occasionally, until the onion softens. Add the celery, carrot, and garlic and cook, covered, for an additional 5 minutes, stirring frequently.

2 Add the water, potato, parsnip, kohlrabi or turnip, and green beans. Bring to a boil, reduce the heat to low and simmer, covered, for 5 minutes.

3 Add the peas, zucchini, and flageolet beans, and season generously with salt and pepper.

Cover again and simmer for about 25 minutes until all the vegetables are tender.

4 Meanwhile, make the pesto. Put the garlic, basil, and cheese in a food processor with the olive oil and process until smooth, scraping down the sides as necessary. Alternatively, pound together using a pestle and mortar.

5 Add the spinach to the soup and simmer for an additional 5 minutes. Taste and adjust the seasoning and stir about a tablespoon of the pesto into the soup. Ladle into warm bowls and pass the remaining pesto separately.

Baked Leek & Cabbage Soup

*A flavorful stock is important for this delicious and filling soup,
which is a typical peasant-style bread soup, perfect for supper.*

Serves 4

INGREDIENTS

2 tbsp. butter

2 large leeks, halved lengthwise and
thinly sliced

1 large onion, halved and thinly sliced

3 garlic cloves, finely chopped

9 oz. finely shredded green cabbage

4 cups chicken or meat stock

4 slices firm bread, cut in half, or

8 slices baguette

9 oz. grated Gruyère cheese

1 Melt the butter in a large saucepan over a medium heat. Add the leeks and onion and cook for 4–5 minutes, stirring frequently, until just softened.

2 Add the garlic and cabbage, stir to combine and continue cooking for about 5 minutes until the cabbage is wilted.

3 Stir in the stock and simmer for 10 minutes. Taste and season with salt and pepper.

4 Arrange the bread in the base of a large, deep, 12 cups ovenproof dish. Sprinkle about half the cheese over the bread.

5 Ladle over the soup and top with the remaining cheese. Bake in a preheated oven at 350° F for 1 hour. Serve at once.

VARIATION

*Add about 2¾ oz. cooked ham
strips, sprinkling them over the
bread before the cheese.*

COOK'S TIP

*A large soufflé dish or
earthenware casserole at least
4 inches deep, or an
enamelled cast-iron casserole,
is good for baking the soup. If
the soup fills the dish to the
top, put a baking tray with
a rim underneath to catch
any overflow.*

Roasted Squash, Sweet Potato, & Garlic Soup

*When there's a chill in the air, this vivid soup is just the thing to serve—
it's very warm and comforting.*

Serves 6

INGREDIENTS

1 sweet potato, about 12 oz.

1 acorn squash

4 shallots

olive oil

5–6 garlic cloves, unpeeled

3¾ cups chicken stock

½ cup light cream

salt and pepper

snipped chives, to garnish

1 Cut the sweet potato, squash, and shallots in half lengthwise, through to the stem end. Brush the cut sides with oil.

2 Put the vegetables, cut sides down, in a shallow roasting pan. Add the garlic cloves. Roast in a preheated oven at 375° F for about 40 minutes until tender and light brown.

3 When cool, scoop the flesh from the potato and squash halves, and put in a saucepan with the shallots. Remove the garlic peel and add the soft insides to the other vegetables.

4 Add the stock and a pinch of salt. Bring just to a boil, reduce the heat and simmer, partially covered, for about 30 minutes, stirring occasionally, until the vegetables are very tender.

5 Allow the soup to cool slightly, then transfer to a blender or food processor and purée until smooth, working in batches, if necessary. (If using a food processor, strain off the cooking liquid and reserve. Purée the soup solids with enough cooking liquid to moisten them, then combine with the remaining liquid.)

6 Return the soup to the saucepan and stir in the cream. Season to taste, then simmer for 5–10 minutes until completely heated through. Ladle into warm bowls to serve.

Celeriac, Leek, & Potato Soup

It is hard to imagine that celeriac, a coarse, knobbly vegetable, can taste so sweet. It makes a wonderfully flavorful soup.

Serves 4

INGREDIENTS

1 tbsp. butter

1 onion, chopped

2 large leeks, halved lengthwise and sliced

1 large celeriac (about 1 lb. 10 oz),

peeled and cubed

1 potato, cubed

1 carrot, quartered and thinly sliced

5 cups water

⅛ tsp. dried marjoram

1 bay leaf

freshly grated nutmeg

salt and pepper

celery leaves, to garnish

1 Melt the butter in a large saucepan over a medium-low heat. Add the onion and leeks and cook for about 4 minutes, stirring frequently, until just softened; do not allow to color.

2 Add the celeriac, potato, carrot, water, marjoram, and bay leaf, with a large pinch of salt. Bring to a boil, reduce the heat, cover and simmer for about 25 minutes until the vegetables are tender. Remove the bay leaf.

3 Allow the soup to cool slightly. Transfer to a blender or food processor and purée until smooth. (If using food processor, strain off cooking liquid and reserve. Purée the soup solids with enough cooking liquid to moisten them, then combine with remaining liquid.)

4 Return the puréed soup to the saucepan and stir to blend. Season with salt, pepper, and nutmeg. Simmer over a medium-low heat until reheated.

5 Ladle the soup into warm bowls, garnish with celery leaves and serve.

Carrot & Almond Soup

Carrots and almonds have a natural affinity that is obvious in this soup.

Serves 4–6

INGREDIENTS

2 tsp. olive oil
1 onion, finely chopped
1 leek, thinly sliced
1 lb. 2 oz. carrots, thinly sliced

6¼ cups water
1¾ oz. soft white breadcrumbs
1½ cups ground almonds
1 tbsp. fresh lemon juice, or to taste

salt and pepper
snipped fresh chives, to garnish

1 Heat the oil in a large saucepan over a medium heat and add the onion and leek. Cover and cook for about 3 minutes, stirring occasionally, until just softened; do not allow them to brown.

2 Add the carrots and water and season with a little salt and pepper. Bring to a boil, reduce the heat and simmer gently, partially covered, for about 45 minutes until the vegetables are tender.

3 Soak the breadcrumbs in cold water to cover for 2–3

minutes, then strain them and press out the remaining water.

4 Put the almonds and breadcrumbs in a blender or food processor with a ladleful of the carrot cooking water and purée until smooth and paste-like.

5 Transfer the soup vegetables and remaining cooking liquid to the blender or food processor and purée until smooth, working in batches if necessary. (If using a food processor, strain off the cooking liquid and reserve. Purée the soup solids with enough cooking liquid

to moisten them, then combine with the remaining liquid.)

6 Return the soup to the saucepan and simmer over a low heat, stirring occasionally, until heated through. Add lemon juice, salt and pepper to taste. Ladle the soup into warm bowls, garnish with chives and serve.

Tarragon Pea Soup

This soup is simple and quick to make using frozen peas and stock made from a cube, ingredients you are likely to have on hand.

Serves 4

INGREDIENTS

2 tsp. butter
1 onion, finely chopped
2 leeks, finely chopped
1 ½ tbsp. white rice

1 lb. 2 oz. frozen peas
4 cups water
1 chicken or vegetable stock cube
½ tsp. dried tarragon

salt and pepper
chopped hard-cooked egg or
croutons, to garnish

1 Melt the butter in a large saucepan over a medium-low heat. Add the onion, leeks, and rice. Cover and cook for about 10 minutes, stirring occasionally, until the vegetables are soft.

2 Add the peas, water, stock cube and tarragon and bring just to a boil. Season with a little pepper. Cover and simmer for about 35 minutes, stirring occasionally, until the vegetables are very tender.

3 Allow the soup to cool slightly, then transfer to a

blender or food processor and purée until smooth, working in batches if necessary. (If using a food processor, strain off the cooking liquid and reserve. Purée the soup solids with enough cooking liquid to moisten them, then combine with the remaining liquid.)

4 Return the puréed soup to the saucepan. Taste and adjust the seasoning, adding plenty of pepper and, if needed, salt. Gently reheat the soup over a low heat for about 10 minutes until hot.

5 Ladle into warm bowls and garnish with egg or croutons.

COOK'S TIP

The rice gives the soup a little extra body, but a small amount of raw or cooked potato would do the same job.

VARIATION

Substitute frozen green beans for the peas and omit the tarragon, replacing it with a little dried thyme and/or marjoram.

Smoky Green Bean Soup

For the most robust flavor, use bacon that has been fairly heavily smoked and has a pronounced taste; for a more delicate soup, use unsmoked bacon.

Serves 4

INGREDIENTS

1 tbsp. oil
3½ oz. lean smoked bacon, finely chopped
1 onion, finely chopped
1–2 garlic cloves, finely chopped or crushed

2 tbsp. all-purpose flour
5 cups water
1 leek, thinly sliced
1 carrot, finely chopped
1 small potato, finely chopped
1 lb. 2 oz. green beans

1 bay leaf
freshly grated nutmeg
salt and pepper
garlic croutons, to garnish

1 Heat the oil in a large wide saucepan over a medium heat. Add the bacon and cook for 8–10 minutes until golden. Remove the bacon from the pan with a slotted spoon and drain on paper towels. Pour off all the fat from the pan.

2 Add the onion and garlic to the pan and cook for about 3 minutes, stirring frequently, until the onion begins to soften.

3 Stir in the flour and continue cooking for 2 minutes. Add half of the water and stir well, scraping the bottom of the pan to mix in the flour.

4 Add the leek, carrot, potato, beans, and bay leaf. Stir in the remaining water and season with salt and pepper. Bring just to a boil, stirring occasionally, reduce the heat and simmer, partially covered, for 35–40 minutes, or until the beans are very tender.

5 Allow the soup to cool slightly, then transfer to a blender or food processor, and purée until smooth, working in batches if necessary. (If using a food processor, strain off the cooking liquid and reserve. Purée the soup solids with enough cooking liquid to moisten them, then combine with the remaining liquid.)

6 Return the soup to the saucepan, add the bacon and simmer over a low heat for a few minutes until heated through, stirring occasionally. Taste and adjust the seasoning, adding nutmeg, pepper and, if needed, more salt. Sprinkle with croutons to serve.

VARIATION

Use frozen green beans instead of fresh if you wish. There is no need to defrost them.

Roasted Mediterranean Vegetable Soup

Roasting the vegetables gives this soup its intense, rich flavor, reminiscent of ratatouille.

Serves 6

INGREDIENTS

2–3 tbsp. olive oil

1 lb. 9 oz. ripe tomatoes, skinned, cored and halved

3 large yellow bell peppers, halved, cored and deseeded

3 zucchini, halved lengthwise

1 small eggplant, halved lengthwise

4 garlic cloves, halved

2 onions, cut into eighths

pinch of dried thyme

4 cups chicken, vegetable or meat stock

½ cup light cream

salt and pepper

shredded basil leaves, to garnish

1 Brush a large shallow baking dish with olive oil. Laying them cut-side down, arrange the tomatoes, bell peppers, zucchini, and eggplant in one layer (use two dishes, if necessary). Tuck the garlic cloves and onion pieces into the gaps and drizzle the vegetables with olive oil. Season lightly with salt and pepper and sprinkle with the thyme.

2 Place in a preheated oven at 375° F and bake, uncovered, for 30–35 minutes, or until soft and browned around the edges. Leave to cool, then scrape out the eggplant flesh and remove the skin from the bell peppers.

3 Working in batches, put the eggplant and bell pepper flesh, together with the zucchini, into a food processor and chop to

the consistency of salsa or pickle; do not purée. Alternatively, place in a bowl and chop together with a knife.

4 Combine the stock and chopped vegetable mixture in a saucepan and simmer over a medium heat for between 20–30 minutes until all the vegetables are tender and the flavors have completely blended.

5 Stir in the cream and simmer over a low heat for about 5 minutes, stirring occasionally until hot. Taste and adjust the seasoning, if necessary. Ladle the soup into warm bowls, garnish with basil and serve.

Sweet & Sour Cabbage Soup

This healthy soup is made with an unusual combination of fruits and vegetables, creating a tantalizing flavor that will keep people guessing.

Serves 4–6

INGREDIENTS

½ cup golden raisins
½ cup orange juice
1 tbsp. olive oil
1 large onion, chopped
3 cups shredded cabbage
2 apples, peeled and diced

½ cup apple juice
14 oz. can peeled tomatoes in juice
1 cup tomato or vegetable juice
3 ½ oz. pineapple flesh, finely
    chopped
5 cups water

2 tsp. wine vinegar
salt and pepper
fresh mint leaves, to garnish

1 Put the golden raisins in a bowl, pour the orange juice over and leave for 15 minutes.

2 Heat the oil in a large saucepan over a medium heat, add the onion, cover and cook for 3–4 minutes, stirring frequently, until it starts to soften. Add the cabbage and cook for an extra 2 minutes; do not allow it to brown.

3 Add the apples and apple juice, cover and cook gently for 5 minutes.

4 Stir in the tomatoes, tomato juice, pineapple, and water. Season with salt and pepper and add the vinegar.

5 Add the golden raisins together with the orange juice soaking liquid. Bring to a boil, reduce the heat and simmer, partially covered, for about 1 hour until the fruit and vegetables are tender.

6 Allow the soup to cool slightly, then transfer to a blender or food processor and purée until smooth, working in batches if necessary. (If using a food processor, strain off the cooking liquid and reserve. Purée the soup solids with enough cooking liquid to moisten them, then combine with the remaining liquid.)

7 Return the soup to the saucepan and simmer gently for about 10 minutes to reheat. Ladle into warm bowls. Garnish with mint leaves and serve immediately.

Creamy Onion & Fava Bean Soup

This soup has well-balanced vegetable flavors and a satisfying crunch from the crispy bacon.
It makes a good lunch, served with crusty bread.

Serves 5–6

INGREDIENTS

1 tbsp. butter
2 tsp. oil
2 large onions, finely chopped
1 leek, thinly sliced
1 garlic clove, crushed
5 cups water

6 tbsp. white rice
1 bay leaf
½ tsp. chopped fresh rosemary
   leaves
½ tsp. chopped fresh thyme leaves
12 oz. fresh or defrosted fava beans

3½ oz. bacon, finely chopped
1 ½ cups milk, plus extra if needed
freshly grated nutmeg
salt and pepper

1 Heat the butter and half the oil in a large saucepan over a medium heat. Add the onions, leek and garlic. Season with salt and pepper and cook for 10–15 minutes, stirring frequently, until the onion is soft.

2 Add the water, rice, and herbs with a large pinch of salt. Bring just to a boil and reduce the heat to low. Cover and simmer for 15 minutes.

3 Add the fava beans, cover again and continue simmering for an additional 15 minutes, or until the vegetables are tender. Remove the bay leaf.

4 Allow the soup to cool a bit, transfer to a blender or food processor and purée until smooth, working in batches if necessary. (If using a food processor, strain off the cooking liquid and reserve. Purée the soup solids with enough cooking liquid to moisten them, then combine with the remaining liquid.)

5 Heat the remaining oil in a small frying pan over a medium-low heat. Add the bacon and cook until crispy, stirring occasionally. Drain on paper towels.

6 Return the soup to the saucepan and stir in the milk, adding a little extra for a thinner soup. Taste and adjust the seasoning, adding salt and pepper to taste and a good grating of nutmeg. Simmer over a low heat for about 10 minutes until heated through, stirring occasionally. Ladle the soup into warm bowls and sprinkle with bacon. Serve immediately.

Parsnip Soup with Ginger & Orange

The exotic flavors give this simple soup a lift. If you wish,
use bought ginger purée instead of grating it; add to taste as the strength varies.

Serves 6

INGREDIENTS

2 tsp. olive oil
1 large onion, chopped
1 large leek, sliced
2 carrots, thinly sliced
1 lb. 12 oz. parsnips, sliced

4 tbsp. grated peeled fresh ginger
2–3 garlic cloves, finely chopped
grated rind of ½ orange
6 cups water
1 cup orange juice

salt and pepper
snipped chives or slivers of scallions,
   to garnish

1 Heat the olive oil in a large saucepan over a medium heat. Add the onion and leek and cook for about 5 minutes, stirring occasionally, until softened,

2 Add the parsnips, carrots, ginger, garlic, grated orange rind, water, and a large pinch of salt. Reduce the heat, cover and simmer for about 40 minutes, stirring occasionally, until the vegetables are very soft.

3 Allow the soup to cool slightly, then transfer to a blender or food processor and purée until smooth, working in batches if necessary. (If using a food processor, strain off the cooking liquid and reserve. Purée the soup solids with enough cooking liquid to moisten them, then combine with the remaining liquid.)

4 Return the soup to the saucepan and stir in the orange juice. Add a little water or more orange juice, if you prefer a thinner consistency. Taste and adjust the seasoning with salt and pepper

5 Then simmer for about 10 minutes to heat through. Ladle into warm bowls, garnish with chives or slivers of scallions and serve.

VARIATION

You could make the soup using equal amounts (1 lb. each) of carrots and parsnips.

Corn & Spinach Soup

Fresh corn retains a little crunch when cooked, adding a pleasing texture to this soup.

Serves 4

INGREDIENTS

3 ears of corn-on-the-cob, cooked
1 tsp. butter
1 tsp. oil
1 large onion, finely chopped
1 leek, thinly sliced
1 carrot, finely chopped

1 large potato, diced
5 cups water
½ cup heavy cream
½ cup milk
freshly grated nutmeg
6 oz. spinach leaves, finely chopped

salt and pepper

1 Cut the kernels from the corn, without cutting all the way down to the cob. Using the back of a knife, scrape the cobs to extract the milky liquid; reserve.

2 Heat the butter and oil in a large saucepan over a medium heat and add the onion and leek. Cover and cook for 3–4 minutes, stirring frequently, until softened.

3 Add the carrot, potato, and water with a large pinch of salt. Bring just to a boil and stir in the corn kernels and the liquid scraped from the cobs. Reduce the heat to low, cover and simmer for about 25 minutes, or until the carrot and potato are tender.

4 Allow the soup to cool slightly, then transfer about half of it to a blender or food processor and purée until smooth.

5 Return the puréed soup to the saucepan, add the cream and milk and stir to blend. Thin with a little more milk, if preferred. Season with salt, pepper and nutmeg. Simmer over a low heat until reheated.

6 Add the spinach and cook for 4–5 minutes, stirring frequently, just until the spinach is completely wilted. Taste and adjust the seasoning, if necessary, then ladle the soup into warm bowls. Serve at once.

COOK'S TIP

To cut corn kernels off the cob, lay on its side on a cutting board and slice lengthwise, rotating until all kernels are removed. Then stand on its stem and scrape down to extract the remaining pulp and juice.

Wild Mushroom Soup

*This soup has an intense, earthy flavor that brings to mind woodland aromas.
It makes a memorable, rich-tasting starter.*

Serves 4

INGREDIENTS

1 oz. dried porcini mushrooms
1½ cups boiling water
4½ oz. fresh porcini mushrooms
2 tsp. olive oil
1 stalk celery, chopped
1 carrot, chopped

1 onion, chopped
3 garlic cloves, crushed
5 cups vegetable stock or water
leaves from 2 thyme sprigs
1 tbsp. butter
3 tbsp. dry or medium sherry

2–3 tbsp. sour cream
salt and pepper
chopped fresh parsley, to garnish

1 Put the dried mushrooms in a bowl and pour the boiling water over them. Allow to stand for 10–15 minutes.

2 Brush or wash the fresh mushrooms. Trim and reserve the stalks; slice large mushroom caps.

3 Heat the oil in a large saucepan over a medium heat. Add the celery, carrot, onion, and mushroom stems. Cook for about 8 minutes, stirring frequently, until the onion begins to color. Stir in the garlic and continue cooling for one minute.

4 Add the stock and thyme leaves with a large pinch of salt. Using a slotted spoon, transfer the soaked dried mushrooms to the saucepan. Strain the soaking liquid through a muslin-lined sieve into the pan. Bring to a boil, reduce the heat and simmer, partially covered, for 30–40 minutes, or until the carrots are tender.

5 Allow the soup to cool slightly, then transfer the soup solids with enough of the cooking liquid to moisten to a blender or food processor and purée until smooth. Return it to the saucepan, combine with the remaining cooking liquid and simmer gently, covered.

6 Melt the butter in a frying pan over a medium heat. Add the fresh mushroom caps and season with salt and pepper. Cook for about 8 minutes until they start to color, stirring occasionally at first, then stirring more often as the liquid evaporates. When the pan becomes dry, add the sherry and bubble briefly.

7 Add the mushrooms and sherry to the soup. Taste and adjust the seasoning, if necessary. Ladle into warm bowls, put a dollop of cream in each and garnish with parsley.

Curried Zucchini Soup

This soup is lightly curried to allow the delicate flavor of the zucchini to come through. If you prefer a more dominant curry taste, add a little more powder.

Serves 4

INGREDIENTS

2 tsp. butter
1 large onion, finely chopped
2 lb. zucchini, sliced

2 cups chicken or vegetable stock
1 tsp. curry powder
½ cup sour cream

salt and pepper

1 Melt the butter in a large saucepan over a medium heat. Add the onion and cook for about 3 minutes until it begins to soften.

2 Add the stock, zucchini, and curry powder, along with a large pinch of salt if using unsalted stock. Bring the soup to a boil, reduce the heat, cover and cook gently for about 25 minutes until the vegetables are tender.

3 Allow the soup to cool slightly, then transfer to a blender or food processor, working in batches if necessary. Purée the soup until just smooth, but still with green flecks. (If using a food processor, strain off the cooking liquid and reserve. Purée the soup solids with enough cooking liquid to moisten them, then combine with the remaining liquid.)

4 Return the soup to the saucepan and stir in the sour cream. Reheat gently over a low heat just until hot. (Do not boil.)

5 Taste and adjust the seasoning, if needed. Ladle into warm bowls and serve.

COOK'S TIP

Stock made from a cube or liquid stock base is fine for this soup. In this case, you may wish to add a little more sour cream. The soup freezes well, but freeze it without the cream and add before serving.

VARIATION

This soup is delicious served cold. Cool and chill the puréed soup. Stir in the sour cream just before serving.

Roasted Garlic & Potato Soup

*The combination of potato, garlic, and onion works brilliantly in soup.
In this recipe the garlic is roasted to give it added dimension and depth.*

Serves 4

INGREDIENTS

1 large bulb. garlic with large cloves,
   peeled (about 3½ oz.)
2 tsp. olive oil
2 large leeks, thinly sliced
1 large onion, finely chopped
3 potatoes, diced (about 1 lb. 2 oz)

5 cups chicken or vegetable stock
1 bay leaf
⅔ cup light cream
freshly grated nutmeg
fresh lemon juice (optional)
salt and pepper

snipped fresh chives, to garnish

1 Put the garlic cloves in a baking dish, lightly brush with oil and bake in a preheated oven at 350° F for about 20 minutes until golden.

2 Heat the oil in a large saucepan over a medium heat. Add the leeks and onion, cover and cook for about 3 minutes, stirring frequently, until they begin to soften.

3 Add the potatoes, roasted garlic, stock, and bay leaf.

Season with salt (unless the stock is salty) and pepper. Bring to a boil, reduce the heat, cover and cook gently for about 30 minutes until the vegetables are tender. Remove the bay leaf.

4 Allow the soup to cool slightly, then transfer to a blender or food processor and purée until smooth, working in batches if necessary. (If using a food processor, strain off the cooking liquid and reserve. Purée the soup solids with enough cooking liquid

to moisten them, then combine with the remaining liquid.)

5 Return the soup to the saucepan and stir in the cream and a generous grating of nutmeg. Taste and adjust the seasoning, if necessary, adding a few drops of lemon juice, if wished. Reheat over a low heat. Ladle into warm soup bowls, garnish with chives or parsley and serve.

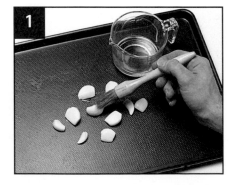

Sweet Potato, Apple, & Leek Soup

This soup makes a marvelous late-autumn or winter starter.
It has a delicious texture and cheerful golden color.

Serves 6

INGREDIENTS

1 tbsp. butter
3 leeks, thinly sliced
1 large carrot, thinly sliced
2 sweet potatoes, peeled and cubed
2 large tart apples, such as Granny

Smiths, peeled and cubed
5 cups water
freshly grated nutmeg
1 cup apple juice
1 cup whipping or light cream

salt and pepper
snipped fresh chives or cilantro,
   to garnish

1 Melt the butter in a large saucepan over a medium-low heat. Add the leeks, cover and cook for 6–8 minutes, or until softened, stirring frequently.

2 Add the carrot, sweet potatoes, apples, and water. Season lightly with salt, pepper and nutmeg. Bring to a boil, reduce the heat and simmer, covered, for about 20 minutes, stirring occasionally, until the vegetables are very tender.

3 Allow the soup to cool slightly, then transfer to a blender or food processor and purée until smooth, working in batches if necessary. (If using a food processor, strain off the cooking liquid and reserve. Purée the soup solids with enough cooking liquid to moisten them, then combine with the remaining liquid.)

4 Return the puréed soup to the saucepan and stir in the apple juice. Place over a low heat

and simmer for about 10 minutes until heated through.

5 Stir in the cream and continue simmering for about 5 minutes, stirring frequently, until heated through. Taste and adjust the seasoning, adding more salt, pepper, and nutmeg, if necessary. Ladle the soup into warm bowls, garnish with chives or cilantro and serve.

Seafood Soups

Soups made from fish and shellfish are enjoyed in almost all parts of the world and provide a satisfying and often more economical way to serve these nutritious foods. They are usually quickly cooked, as well.

Stew-like fisherman's soups were developed to utilize the unsold catch and traditionally contain a variety of fish and shellfish. They are well suited to substitution and improvisation. Feel free to use whatever seafood is fresh and seasonal.

Although many of the soups in this chapter do not require fish stock, it may be used instead of water to give more fish flavor, if you have it handy. Mussels and clams yield a delicious liquid when cooked that lends much flavor to soups. The shells of shrimp and other crustaceans make delicious stock as well. Fish stock takes less time to make than other stocks and a basic recipe can be found in this chapter (see page 102). Diluted chicken stock may be substituted for fish stock in a pinch.

Seafood soups range from the very simple—broth with shellfish—to diverse combinations with exotic seasonings. The following recipes offer ample opportunity to explore a variety of soups made from fish and shellfish.

Seared Scallops in Garlic Broth

This soup is both simple and very elegant.
Its lightness makes it particularly suitable as a starter.

Serves 4

INGREDIENTS

5 cups water
1 large garlic bulb. (about 3½ oz.),
    separated into unpeeled cloves
1 stalk celery, chopped
1 carrot, chopped

1 onion, chopped
10 peppercorns
5–6 parsley stems
1 tbsp. oil
8 oz. large sea scallops

or queen scallops
salt and pepper
cilantro, to garnish

---

1 Combine the garlic cloves, celery, carrot, onion, peppercorns, parsley stems, and water in a saucepan with a good pinch of salt. Bring to a boil, reduce the heat and simmer, partially covered, for 30–45 minutes.

2 Strain the stock into a clean saucepan. Taste and adjust the seasoning, and keep hot.

3 If using sea scallops, slice in half to form 2 thinner rounds

from each. (If the scallops are very large, slice them into 3 rounds.) Sprinkle with salt and pepper.

4 Heat the oil in a frying pan over a medium-high heat and cook the scallops on one side for 1–2 minutes until lightly browned and the flesh becomes opaque.

5 Divide the scallops between 4 warm shallow bowls, arranging them browned-side up. Ladle the soup over the scallops, then float a few cilantro leaves on

top. Serve at once.

VARIATION

Use fish stock instead of water to make the garlic stock if you want a more fishy flavor, or add Asian fish sauce, such as nam pla, to taste.

Saffron Mussel Soup

*Mussels are easy to prepare, economical and very tasty. This soup has pure,
delicate flavors and the fresh aromas of the sea.*

Serves 4–6

INGREDIENTS

4 lb. 8 oz. mussels
⅔ cup dry white wine
1 tbsp. butter
2 large shallots, finely chopped
1 leek, halved lengthwise and thinly

sliced
pinch of saffron threads
1 ¼ cups heavy cream
1 tbsp. cornstarch, dissolved in 2 tbsp.
water

salt and pepper
2 tbsp. chopped fresh parsley

1 Discard any broken mussels and those with open shells that do not close when tapped. Rinse, pull off any "beards," and if there are barnacles, scrape them off with a knife under cold running water.

2 Put the mussels in a large heavy-based saucepan over a high heat with the wine and a little pepper. Cover tightly and cook for 4–5 minutes, or until the mussels open, shaking the pan occasionally.

3 When they are cool enough to handle, remove the mussels from the shells, adding any additional juices to the cooking liquid. Strain the cooking liquid through a muslin-lined sieve. Top up the cooking liquid with water to make 4 cups.

4 Melt the butter in heavy-based saucepan. Add the shallots and leek, cover and cook until they begin to soften, stirring occasionally.

5 Stir in the mussel cooking liquid and the saffron. Bring to a boil, reduce the heat and simmer for 15–20 minutes until the vegetables are very tender.

6 Add the cream, stir and bring just to a boil. Stir the dissolved cornstarch into the soup and boil gently for 2–3 minutes until slightly thickened, stirring frequently. Add the mussels and cook for 1–2 minutes to reheat them. Taste and adjust the seasoning, if necessary. Stir in the parsley, ladle into warm bowls and serve.

Shellfish & Tomato Soup

*This soup is swimming with seafood. Depending on availability,
you could substitute skinless, boneless white fish for the scallops or shrimp.*

Serves 4–6

INGREDIENTS

2 lb. 4 oz. mussels
2 tbsp. butter
2 shallots, finely chopped
4 tbsp. all-purpose flour
4 tbsp. dry white wine
2½ cups fish stock

7 oz. bay scallops
7 oz. cooked peeled shrimp
½ cup heavy cream
4 tomatoes, skinned, deseeded and
    chopped
2 tbsp. snipped fresh chives

2 tbsp. chopped fresh parsley
salt and pepper

1 Discard any broken mussels and those with open shells that do not close when tapped. Rinse, pull off any "beard," and if there are barnacles, scrape them off with a knife under cold running water. Put the mussels in a large heavy-based saucepan, cover tightly and cook for 4–5 minutes, or until the mussels open, shaking the pan occasionally.

2 When they are cool enough to handle, remove the mussels from the shells, adding additional juices to the cooking liquid. Strain the liquid through a muslin-lined sieve. Top it up with water to make 2 cups.

3 Melt the butter in a large saucepan over a medium-low heat. Add the shallots and cook for 3–4 minutes, stirring frequently, until soft. Stir in the flour and continue cooking for 2 minutes. Add the wine.

4 Slowly add the fish stock and stir well, scraping the bottom of the pan to mix in the flour. Pour in the remaining mussel cooking liquid and water and bring just to a boil, stirring frequently. Reduce the heat, cover and simmer for 10 minutes.

5 Add the scallops, shrimp and mussels, and continue cooking for 1 minute.

6 Stir in the cream, tomatoes, chives, lemon juice, and parsley. Season to taste with salt. Sprinkle with parsley and serve.

Clam & Corn Chowder

Fresh clams make this chowder that bit more special, but they can be expensive. Canned baby clams or razor shell clams can be used instead, turning this soup into a handy instant meal.

Serves 4

INGREDIENTS

1 lb. 10 oz. clams, or 10 oz. can clams
2 tbsp. dry white wine (if needed)
4 tsp. butter
1 large onion, finely chopped
1 small carrot, finely diced
3 tbsp. all-purpose flour

1¼ cups fish stock
¾ cup water (if needed)
1 lb. potatoes, diced
1 cup cooked or defrosted frozen corn
2 cups whole milk

salt and pepper
chopped fresh parsley, to garnish

1 If using fresh clams, put them into a heavy-based saucepan with the wine. Cover tightly, set over a medium-high heat and cook for 2–4 minutes, or until they open, shaking the pan occasionally. Remove the clams from the shells and strain the cooking liquid through a very fine mesh sieve; reserve both. If using canned clams, drain and rinse well.

2 Melt the butter in a large saucepan over a medium-low heat. Add the onion and carrot and cook for 3–4 minutes, stirring frequently, until the onion is softened. Stir in the flour and continue cooking for 2 minutes.

3 Slowly add about half the stock and stir well, scraping the bottom of the pan to mix in the flour. Pour in the remaining stock and the reserved clam cooking liquid, or the water if using canned clams, and bring just to a boil, stirring.

4 Add the potatoes, sweetcorn and milk and stir to combine. Reduce the heat and simmer gently, partially covered, for about 20 minutes, stirring occasionally, until all the vegetables are tender.

5 Chop the clams, if large. Stir in the clams and continue cooking for about 5 minutes until heated through. Taste and adjust the seasoning, if needed.

6 Ladle the soup into bowls and sprinkle with parsley.

Provençal Fish Soup

For the best results, you need to use flavorful fish, such as cod or haddock, for this recipe.
Frozen fish fillets are suitable, and there's no need to defrost them before cooking.

Serves 4–6

INGREDIENTS

1 tbsp. olive oil
2 onions, finely chopped
1 small leek, thinly sliced
1 small carrot, finely chopped
1 stalk celery, finely chopped
1 small fennel bulb, finely chopped
  (optional)

3 garlic cloves, finely chopped
1 cup dry white wine
5 cups water
14 oz. can tomatoes in juice
1 bay leaf
pinch of fennel seeds
2 strips orange rind

¼ tsp. saffron threads
12 oz. skinless white fish fillets
salt and pepper
garlic croutons, to serve (see page 42)

1 Heat the oil in a large saucepan over a medium heat. Add the onions and cook for about 5 minutes, stirring frequently, until softened. Add the leek, carrot, celery, fennel, garlic, and continue cooking for 4–5 minutes until the leek is wilted.

2 Add the wine and let it bubble for a minute. Add the tomatoes, bay leaf, fennel seeds, orange rind, saffron, and water. Bring just to a boil, reduce the heat, cover and cook gently, stirring occasionally, for 30 minutes.

3 Add the fish and cook for an additional 20–30 minutes until it is very soft and flaky. Remove the bay leaf and orange rind if possible.

4 Allow the soup to cool slightly, then transfer to a blender or food processor and purée until smooth, working in batches if necessary. (If using a food processor, strain off the cooking liquid and reserve. Purée the soup solids with enough cooking liquid to moisten them, then combine with the remaining liquid.)

5 Return the soup to the saucepan. Taste and adjust the seasoning, if necessary, and simmer for 5–10 minutes until heated through. Ladle the soup into warm bowls and sprinkle with croutons.

Fennel & Tomato Soup with Shrimp

This light and refreshing soup is also good served cold.
An ideal starter for a summer meal, served with crunchy Melba toast.

Serves 4

INGREDIENTS

2 tsp. olive oil
1 large onion, halved and sliced
2 large fennel bulbs, halved and sliced
1 small potato, diced
3¾ cups water

1⅔ cups tomato juice
1 bay leaf
4½ oz. cooked peeled small shrimp
2 tomatoes, skinned, deseeded and
  chopped

½ tsp. snipped fresh dill
salt and pepper
dill sprigs or fennel fronds, to garnish

1 Heat the olive oil in a large saucepan over a medium heat. Add the onion and fennel and cook for 3–4 minutes, stirring occasionally, until the onion is just softened.

2 Add the potato, water, tomato juice and bay leaf with a large pinch of salt. Reduce the heat, cover and simmer for about 25 minutes, stirring once or twice, until the vegetables are soft.

3 Allow the soup to cool slightly, then transfer to a blender or food processor and purée until smooth, working in batches if necessary. (If using a food processor, strain off the cooking liquid and reserve. Purée the soup solids with enough cooking liquid to moisten them, then combine with the remaining liquid.)

4 Return the soup to the saucepan and add the shrimp.

Simmer gently for about 10 minutes, to reheat the soup and allow it to absorb the shrimp flavor.

5 Stir in the tomatoes and dill. Taste and adjust the seasoning, adding salt, if needed, and pepper. Thin the soup with a little more tomato juice, if wished. Ladle into warm bowls, garnish with dill or fennel fronds and serve.

Seafood Chowder

Mussels, an economical choice at the fish market, give essential flavor to this soup.
The proportions of fish and shrimp are flexible—use more or less as you wish.

Serves 6

INGREDIENTS

2 lb. 4 oz. mussels
4 tbsp. all-purpose flour
6¼ cups fish stock
1 tbsp. butter
1 large onion, finely chopped

12 oz. skinless white fish fillets, such
   as cod, sole or haddock
7 oz. cooked or raw peeled shrimp
1¼ cups whipping cream or heavy
   cream

salt and pepper
snipped fresh dill, to garnish

---

1 Discard any broken mussels and those with open shells that do not close when tapped. Rinse, pull off any "beards," and if there are barnacles, scrape them off with a knife under cold running water. Put the mussels in a large heavy-based saucepan. Cover tightly and cook over a high heat for about 4 minutes, or until the mussels open, shaking the pan occasionally. When they are cool enough to handle, remove the mussels from the shells, adding any additional juices to the cooking liquid. Strain the cooking liquid through a muslin-lined sieve and reserve.

2 Put the flour in a mixing bowl and very slowly whisk in enough of the stock to make a thick paste. Whisk in a little more stock to make a smooth liquid.

3 Melt the butter in heavy-based saucepan over a medium-low heat. Add the onion, cover and cook for about 5 minutes, stirring frequently, until it softens.

4 Add the remaining fish stock and bring to a boil. Slowly whisk in the flour mixture until well combined and bring back to a boil, whisking constantly. Add the mussel cooking liquid. Season with salt, if needed, and pepper. Reduce the heat and simmer, partially covered, for 15 minutes.

5 Add the fish and mussels and continue simmering, stirring occasionally, for about 5 minutes, or until the fish is cooked and begins to flake.

6 Stir in the shrimp and cream. Taste and adjust the seasoning. Simmer for a few minutes longer to heat through. Ladle into warm bowls, sprinkle with dill and serve.

Smoked Haddock & Potato Soup

This chunky aromatic soup is perfect for a cold weather lunch or supper served with crusty bread and a salad.

Serves 4

INGREDIENTS

1 tbsp. oil
2 oz. bacon, cut into thin matchsticks
1 large onion, finely chopped
2 tbsp. all-purpose flour

4 cups milk
1 lb. 9 oz. potatoes, cut into ½ inch cubes
6 oz. skinless smoked haddock

salt and pepper
finely chopped fresh parsley, to garnish

1 Heat the oil in a large saucepan over a medium heat. Add the bacon and cook for 2 minutes. Stir in the onion and continue cooking for 5–7 minutes, stirring frequently, until the onion is soft and the bacon golden. Tip the pan and spoon off as much fat as possible.

2 Stir in the flour and continue cooking for 2 minutes. Add half of the milk and stir well, scraping the bottom of the pan to mix in the flour.

3 Add the potatoes and remaining milk and season with pepper. Bring just to a boil, stirring frequently, then reduce the heat and simmer, partially covered, for 10 minutes.

4 Add the fish and continue cooking, stirring occasionally, for about 15 minutes, or until the potatoes are tender and the fish breaks up easily.

5 Taste the soup and adjust the seasoning (salt may not be needed). Ladle into a warm tureen or bowls and sprinkle generously with chopped parsley.

COOK'S TIP

Cutting the potatoes into small cubes not only looks attractive, but it allows them to cook more quickly and evenly.

Crab Soup

This rich, tasty soup is simple to make and always popular. If you are feeling generous, increase the amount of crab meat for a more luxurious soup.

Serves 4–6

INGREDIENTS

12 oz. crab meat

4 tbsp. butter

1 cup milk

1 large shallot, very finely chopped

4 tbsp. all-purpose flour

1¼ cups fish stock

1¼ cups whipping or heavy cream

4 tbsp. dry Oloroso sherry, or to taste

finely chopped fresh parsley, to garnish

1 Pick over the crab meat to remove any bits of shell. Melt 1 tablespoon of the butter in a small saucepan over a very low heat. Add the crab meat, stir gently and add half the milk. Heat until bubbles appear around the edge and steam rises. Remove from the heat and set aside.

2 Melt the remaining butter in a large saucepan over a low heat. Add the shallot and cook gently for about 10 minutes until softened, stirring frequently; do not allow it to brown.

3 Stir in the flour and cook for 2 minutes. Whisk in the stock and remaining milk and bring to a boil, stirring constantly.

4 Gradually stir in the cream and season with salt and pepper to taste. Reduce the heat and simmer gently, stirring occasionally, for 10–15 minutes, until the shallots are soft and the soup is smooth and thick.

5 Stir in the crab meat mixture. If a thinner soup is preferred, add a little more stock or milk.

Stir in the sherry and simmer for about 5 minutes until heated through. Taste and adjust the seasoning, if necessary. Ladle the soup into warm bowls and garnish with parsley.

VARIATIONS

If you have crab shells, you could make stock with them as described for Lobster Bisque (see page 206) and use in place of the fish stock and half of the milk.

Shrimp Bisque

This soup utilizes every part of the shrimp. If you wish, you could even leave the shrimp flesh out of the soup because most of the flavor comes from the shells.

Serves 4–5

INGREDIENTS

1 lb. 2 oz. cooked shrimp in the shell
2 tsp. oil
2 large onions, halved and sliced
1 carrot, grated
1 stalk celery, sliced
1–2 garlic cloves, finely chopped or

crushed
6¼ cups water
1 bay leaf
2 tsp. butter
6 tbsp. white rice
1 tbsp. tomato paste

fresh lemon juice
salt and pepper
snipped fresh dill or chopped parsley,
    to garnish

1 Peel the shrimp and keep the shells for the soup. Reserve the shrimp flesh, covered, in the refrigerator.

2 Heat the oil in a large saucepan. Add the shrimp shells and cook over a high heat, stirring frequently, until they start to brown. Reduce the heat and add one-quarter of the onions, the carrot, celery and garlic. Cover and cook for 4–5 minutes, stirring frequently, until the onions soften. Add the water and bay leaf

with a small pinch of salt. Bring to a boil, reduce the heat, cover and simmer gently for 25 minutes. Strain the shrimp stock.

3 Heat the butter in a large saucepan over a medium heat and add the remaining onions. Cover and cook for 5–6 minutes, stirring frequently, until they soften and just begin to color. Add the shrimp stock, rice and tomato paste. Bring to a boil. Reduce the heat, cover and simmer for 30 minutes, or until rice is very soft.

4 Allow the soup to cool slightly, then transfer to a blender or food processor and purée until smooth, working in batches if necessary. (If using a food processor, strain off the cooking liquid and reserve. Purée the soup solids with enough cooking liquid to moisten them, then combine with the remaining liquid.)

5 Return the soup to the saucepan and place over a medium-low heat. Add the reserved shrimp and a few drops of lemon juice, or to taste. Simmer for about 8 minutes, stirring occasionally, until the soup is reheated. Taste and adjust the seasoning if necessary. Ladle into warm bowls, sprinkle with dill or parsley and serve.

Thai-style Seafood Soup

As taste and tolerance for chilies varies, using chili paste offers more control of the heat.
If you are used to cooking with chilies, use one in the stock infusion instead of the paste.

Serves 4

INGREDIENTS

5 cups fish stock
1 lemon grass stalk, split lengthwise
pared rind of ½ lime, or 1 lime leaf
1 inch piece fresh ginger, peeled and
   sliced

¼ tsp. chili paste, or to taste
4–6 scallions, sliced
7 oz. large of medium raw shrimp,
   peeled
9 oz. scallops (16–20 pieces)

2 tbsp. cilantro
salt
finely chopped red bell pepper, or red
   chili rings, to garnish

1 Put the stock in a saucepan with the lemon grass, lime rind or leaf, ginger, and chili paste. Bring just to a boil, reduce the heat, cover and simmer for 10–15 minutes.

2 Cut the baby leek in half lengthwise, then slice crossways very thinly. Cut the shrimp almost in half lengthwise, keeping the tail intact.

3 Strain the stock, return to the saucepan and bring to a simmer, with bubbles rising at the edges and the surface trembling. Add the leek and cook for 2–3 minutes. Taste and season with salt, if needed, and stir in a little more chili paste if wished.

4 Add the scallops and shrimp and poach for about 1 minute until they turn opaque and the shrimp curl.

5 Drop in the cilantro, ladle the soup into warm bowls, dividing the shellfish evenly, and garnish with red bell pepper or chilies.

COOK'S TIP

If you have light chicken stock, but no fish stock, it will make an equally tasty though different version of this soup.

VARIATION

Substitute very small baby leeks, slivered or thinly sliced diagonally, for the scallions. Include the green parts for color.

Salmon & Leek Soup

Salmon is a favorite with almost everyone. This delicately flavored and pretty soup is perfect for entertaining.

Serves 4

INGREDIENTS

1 tbsp. olive oil
1 large onion, finely chopped
3 large leeks, including green parts, thinly sliced
1 potato, finely diced
2 cups fish stock

3 cups water
1 bay leaf
10½ oz. skinless salmon fillet, cut into ½ inch cubes
⅓ cup heavy cream
salt and pepper

fresh lemon juice (optional)
snipped fresh chervil or parsley, to garnish

1 Heat the oil in a heavy-based saucepan over a medium heat. Add the onion and leeks and cook for about 3 minutes until they begin to soften.

2 Add the potato, stock, water, and bay leaf with a large pinch of salt. Bring to a boil, reduce the heat, cover and cook gently for about 25 minutes until the vegetables are tender. Remove the bay leaf.

3 Allow the soup to cool slightly, then transfer about half of it to a blender or food processor and purée until smooth. (If using a food processor, strain off the cooking liquid and reserve. Purée half the soup solids with enough cooking liquid to moisten them, then combine with the remaining liquid.)

4 Return the puréed soup to the saucepan and stir to blend. Reheat gently over a medium-low heat.

5 Season the salmon with salt and pepper and add to the soup. Continue cooking for about 5 minutes, stirring occasionally, until the fish is tender and starts to break up. Stir in the cream, taste and adjust the seasoning, adding a little lemon juice if wished. Ladle into warm bowls, sprinkle with chervil or parsley and serve.

Caribbean Green Seafood Soup

This pretty soup is packed with exotic flavors. It is traditionally made with the roots and leaves of local tuberous vegetables, but potato and spinach make a practical alternative.

Serves 4–6

INGREDIENTS

5½ oz. peeled medium shrimp

7 oz. skinless firm white fish fillets, cubed

¾ tsp. ground coriander

¼ tsp. ground cumin

1 tsp. chili paste, or to taste

3 tbsp. fresh lemon juice, or to taste

1 tbsp. butter

1 onion, halved and thinly sliced

2 large leeks, thinly sliced

3 garlic cloves, finely chopped

1 large potato, diced

5 cups chicken or vegetable stock

9 oz. spinach leaves

½ cup coconut milk

salt and pepper

1 Put the shrimp and fish in a bowl with the coriander, cumin, chili paste, and lemon juice and leave to marinate.

2 Melt the butter in a large saucepan over a medium heat. Add the onion and leeks, cover and cook for about 10 minutes, stirring occasionally, until they are soft. Add the garlic and cook for an additional 3–4 minutes.

3 Add the potato and stock, together with a large pinch of salt, if using unsalted stock. Bring to a boil, reduce the heat, cover and cook gently for 15–20 minutes until the potato is tender. Stir in the spinach and continue cooking, uncovered, for about 3 minutes until it is just wilted.

4 Allow the soup to cool slightly, then transfer to a blender or food processor, working in batches if necessary. Purée the soup until smooth. (If using a food processor, strain off the cooking liquid and reserve. Purée the soup solids with enough cooking liquid to moisten them, then combine with the remaining liquid.)

5 Return the soup to the saucepan and stir in the coconut milk. Add the fish and shrimp with their marinade. Simmer over a medium-low heat for about 8 minutes, stirring frequently, until the soup is heated through and the fish is cooked and flakes easily.

6 Taste and adjust the seasoning, adding more chili paste and/or lemon juice if wished. Ladle into warm bowls and serve.

VARIATION

Add a handful of cilantro to the spinach.

Squid, Chorizo, & Tomato Soup

This soup is full of interesting flavors. The chorizo gives it appealing spicy undertones that marry well with the savory squid.

Serves 6

INGREDIENTS

1 lb. cleaned squid

5 ½ oz. lean chorizo, peeled and very finely diced

1 onion, finely chopped

1 stalk celery, thinly sliced

1 carrot, thinly sliced

2 garlic cloves, finely chopped or crushed

14 oz. can chopped tomatoes in juice

5 cups fish stock

½ tsp. ground cumin

pinch of saffron

1 bay leaf

salt and pepper

chili paste (optional)

fresh parsley, chopped

1 Cut off the squid tentacles and cut into bite-sized pieces. Slice the bodies into rings.

2 Place a large saucepan over a medium-low heat and add the chorizo. Cook for 5–10 minutes, stirring frequently, until it renders most of its fat. Remove with a slotted spoon and drain on paper towels.

3 Pour off all the fat from the pan and add the onion, celery, carrot and garlic. Cover and cook for 3–4 minutes until the onion is slightly softened.

4 Stir in the tomatoes, fish stock, cumin, saffron, bay leaf, and chorizo.

5 Add the squid to the soup. Bring almost to a boil, reduce the heat, cover and cook gently for 40–45 minutes, or until the squid and carrot are tender, stirring occasionally.

6 Taste the soup and stir in a little chili paste for a spicier flavor, if wished. Season with salt and pepper. Ladle into warm bowls, sprinkle with parsley and serve.

VARIATION

Ready-cooked squid rings can be used in place of whole squid, but they may not have as much flavor. If using, reduce cooking time by about 20 minutes.

COOK'S TIP

Chorizo varies varies in the amount of fat and the degree of spiciness. A lean style is best for this soup.

Breton Fish Soup with Cider & Sorrel

Fishermen's soups are inevitably variable, depending on the season and the catch.
Monkfish, has a texture like lobster, but tender cod is an equally appealing.

Serves 4

INGREDIENTS

2 tsp. butter
1 large leek, thinly sliced
2 shallots, finely chopped
½ cup hard cider
1¼ cups fish stock

9 oz. potatoes, diced
1 bay leaf
4 tbsp. all-purpose flour
¾ cup milk
¾ cup double heavy cream

2 oz. fresh sorrel leaves
12 oz. skinless monkfish or cod fillet,
   cut into 1 inch pieces
salt and pepper

1 Melt the butter in a large saucepan over a medium-low heat. Add the leek and shallots and cook for about 5 minutes, stirring frequently, until they start to soften. Add the cider and bring to a boil.

2 Stir in the stock, potatoes and bay leaf with a laregg pinch of salt (unless stock is salty) and bring back to a boil. Reduce the heat, cover and cook gently for 10 minutes.

3 Put the flour in a small bowl and very slowly whisk in a few tablespoons of the milk to make a thick paste. Stir in a little more to make a smooth liquid.

4 Adjust the heat so the soup bubbles gently. Stir in the flour mixture and cook, stirring frequently, for 5 minutes. Add the remaining milk and half the cream. Continue cooking for about 10 minutes until the potatoes are tender.

5 Chop the sorrel finely and combine with the remaining cream. (If using a food processor, add the sorrel and chop, then add the cream and process briefly.)

6 Stir the sorrel cream into the soup and add the fish. Continue cooking, stirring occasionally, for about 3 minutes, until the monkfish stiffens or the cod just begins to flake. Taste the soup and adjust the seasoning, if needed. Ladle into warm bowls and serve.

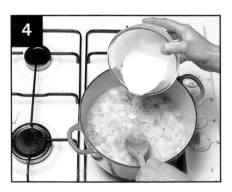

COOK'S TIP

Be careful not to overcook the fish,
otherwise tender fish, such as cod,
break up into smaller and smaller
flakes and firm fish, like monkfish,
can become tough.

Saffron Fish Soup

This elegant soup makes a good dinner party starter. To make planning easier, the saffron-flavored soup base can be made ahead and the fish can then be cooked at the last moment.

Serves 4

INGREDIENTS

2 tsp. butter
1 onion, finely chopped
1 leek, thinly sliced
1 carrot, thinly sliced
4 tbsp. white rice
pinch of saffron threads

½ cup dry white wine
½ cup heavy cream
12 oz. skinless white fish fillet, such
    as cod, haddock, or monkfish, cut
    into ½ inch cubes
4 cups fish stock

4 tomatoes, skinned, deseeded, and
    chopped
3 tbsp. snipped fresh chives, to garnish
salt and pepper

1 Heat the butter in a saucepan over a medium heat and add the onion, leek, and carrot. Cook for 3–4 minutes, stirring frequently, until the onion is soft.

2 Add the saffron, rice, wine and stock, bring just to a boil and reduce the heat to low. Season with salt and pepper. Cover and simmer for 20 minutes, or until the rice and vegetables are soft.

3 Allow the soup to cool slightly, then transfer to a

blender or food processor and purée until smooth, working in batches if necessary. (If using a food processor, strain off the cooking liquid and reserve. Purée the soup solids with enough cooking liquid to moisten them, then combine with the remaining liquid.)

4 Return the soup to the saucepan, stir in the cream and simmer over a low heat for a few minutes until heated through, stirring occasionally.

5 Season the fish and add, with the tomatoes, to the simmering soup. Cook for 3–5 minutes, or until the fish is just tender.

6 Stir in most of the chives. Taste the soup and adjust the seasoning, if necessary. Ladle into warm shallow bowls, sprinkle the remaining chilies on top and serve.

Garlic Fish Soup

The delicate color of this soup belies its heady flavors. The recipe has been adapted from a classic French soup thickened with a garlic mayonnaise.

Serves 4–5

INGREDIENTS

2 tsp. olive oil
1 large onion, chopped
1 small fennel bulb, chopped
1 leek, sliced
3–4 large garlic cloves, thinly sliced
½ cup dry white wine

5 cups fish stock
4 tbsp. white rice
1 strip pared lemon rind
1 bay leaf
1 lb. skinless white fish fillets, cut into
   1½ inch pieces

¼ cup heavy cream
2 tbsp. chopped fresh parsley
salt and pepper

1 Heat the oil in a large saucepan over a medium-low heat. Add the onion, fennel, leek and garlic and cook for 4–5 minutes, stirring frequently, until the onion is softened.

2 Add the wine and bubble briefly. Add the stock, rice, lemon rind and bay leaf. Bring to a boil, reduce the heat to medium-low and simmer for 20–25 minutes, or until the rice and vegetables are soft. Remove the lemon rind and bay leaf.

3 Allow the soup to cool slightly, then transfer to a blender or food processor and purée until smooth, working in batches if necessary. (If using a food processor, strain off the cooking liquid and reserve. Purée the soup solids with enough cooking liquid to moisten them, then combine with the remaining liquid.)

4 Return the soup to the saucepan and bring to a simmer. Add the fish to the soup, cover and continue simmering gently, stirring occasionally, for 4–5 minutes, or until the fish is cooked and begins to flake.

5 Stir in the cream. Taste and adjust the seasoning, adding salt, if needed, and pepper. Ladle into warm bowls and serve sprinkled with parsley.

Curried Tuna Chowder

This tasty soup uses canned tuna and tomatoes, two pantry favorites that you are likely to have on hand, for a quickly made lunch or supper.

Serves 3–4

INGREDIENTS

7 oz. can light meat tuna packed in
 water

1½ tbsp. butter

1 onion, finely chopped

1 garlic clove, finely chopped

2 tbsp. all-purpose flour

2 tsp. mild curry powder

14 oz. can plum tomatoes in juice

3 tbsp. white rice

1 zucchini, finely diced

½ cup single cream

salt and pepper

1 Drain the tuna over a measuring cup and add boiling water to make up to 2 ½ cups.

2 Melt the butter in a large saucepan over a medium-low heat. Add the onion and garlic and cook for about 5 minutes until the onion is softened, stirring frequently.

3 Stir in the flour and curry powder. Continue cooking for 2 minutes.

4 Slowly add about half of the tuna juice and water mixture and stir well, scraping the bottom of the pan to mix in the flour. Pour in the remaining mixture and bring just to a boil, stirring frequently. Add the tomatoes and break up with a spoon. When the soup almost comes back to a boil, stir in the rice, reduce the heat, cover and simmer for 10 minutes.

5 Add the tuna and zucchini and continue cooking for about 15 minutes,

or until the vegetables and rice are tender.

6 Stir in the cream, season with salt and pepper to taste and continue simmering for 3–4 minutes until heated through. Ladle into warm bowls and serve.

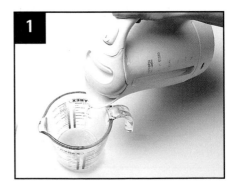

Mussel, Potato, & Parsley Soup

This soup can be made in stages, so is well suited for entertaining.

Serves 4

INGREDIENTS

2 lb. 4 oz. mussels
10½ oz. potatoes
3 tbsp. all-purpose flour
2½ cups milk

1¼ cups whipping cream
1–2 garlic cloves, finely chopped
6 cups curly parsley leaves (1 large bunch)

salt and pepper

1 Discard any broken mussels and those with open shells that do not close when tapped. Rinse under cold running water, pull off any "beards," and scrape off barnacles with a knife. Put the mussels in a large heavy-based saucepan. Cover tightly and cook over a high heat for about 4 minutes, or until the mussels open.

2 When cool enough to handle, remove the mussels from the shells, adding any additional juices to the cooking liquid. Strain the cooking liquid into a bowl through a muslin-lined sieve and put aside.

3 Boil the potatoes, in their skins, in salted water for about 15 minutes until tender. When cool enough to handle, peel and cut into small dice.

4 Put the flour in a mixing bowl and very slowly whisk in a few tablespoons of the milk to make a thick paste. Stir in a little more to make a smooth liquid.

5 Put the remaining milk, cream and garlic in a saucepan and bring to a boil. Whisk in the flour mixture. Reduce the heat to medium-low and simmer for about 15 minutes

until the garlic is tender and the liquid has thickened slightly. Drop in the parsley leaves and cook for about 2–3 minutes until bright green and wilted.

6 Allow the soup base to cool slightly, then transfer to a blender or food processor and purée until smooth, working in batches if necessary. (If using a food processor, strain off the cooking liquid and reserve. Purée the soup solids with enough cooking liquid to moisten, then combine with the remaining liquid.)

7 Return the purée to the saucepan and stir in the mussel cooking liquid and the potatoes. Season to taste with salt, if needed, and pepper. Simmer the soup gently for 5–7 minutes until reheated. Add the mussels and continue cooking for about 2 minutes until the soup is steaming and the mussels are hot. Ladle the soup into warm bowls and serve.

Trout & Celeriac Soup

The cooking liquid in which the fish is poached becomes a delicious fish stock.
If you just want stock, poach fish heads and trimmings instead of a whole fish.

Serves 4–6

INGREDIENTS

1 lb. 9 oz. whole trout
7 oz. celeriac, peeled and diced
¼ cup heavy cream
3 tbsp. cornstarch, dissolved in 3 tbsp.
   water
chopped fresh chervil or parsley, to
   garnish

FISH STOCK BASE:
1 tbsp. butter
I onion, thinly sliced
I carrot, thinly sliced
I leek, thinly sliced
I cup dry white wine

5 cups water
1 bay leaf

1 To make the fish stock base, melt the butter in a fish kettle, a large saucepan or cast-iron casserole over a medium-high heat. Add the onion, carrot, and leek and cook for about 3 minutes, or until the onion starts to soften.

2 Add the wine, water, and bay leaf. Bring to a boil, reduce the heat a little, cover and boil gently for 15 minutes.

3 Put the fish into the liquid (if necessary, cut the fish in

pieces to fit in). Bring back to the boil and skim off any foam that rises to the top. Reduce the heat to low and simmer gently for 20 minutes.

4 Remove the fish and set aside. Strain the stock through a muslin-lined sieve into a clean saucepan. Remove any fat from the stock. (There should be about 6 cups stock.)

5 Bring the stock to a boil. Add the celeriac and boil gently,

uncovered, for 15–20 minutes until it is tender and the liquid has reduced by about one-third.

6 When the fish is cool enough to handle, peel off the skin, and remove the flesh from the bones. Discard the skin, bones, head, and tail.

7 Add the cream to the soup and when it comes back to a boil, stir in the dissolved cornstarch. Boil gently for 2–3 minutes until slightly thickened, stirring frequently. Return the fish to the soup. Cook for 3–4 minutes to reheat. Taste and adjust the seasoning, if necessary. Ladle into warm bowls and garnish with chervil or parsley.

Meat & Poultry Soups

Soups made from meat and poultry range from the lightest consommés to the most substantial meal-in-a-bowl creations, as well as everything in between. Meat and poultry soups offer an almost unlimited variety of choices, from a simple chicken broth with pasta to beefy soup-stews to exotically flavored Asian soups.

Many of the soups that follow offer real nourishment and are perfect served as a main course, accompanied by bread and perhaps a salad or cheese. Such soups can provide a balanced serving of protein, vegetables, and carbohydrates all in one dish for a wholesome and uncomplicated meal.

For the most part, meat and poultry soups call for stock, or they make their own stock during the cooking process. You will find recipes for both beef and chicken stock on pages 108 and 128 of this chapter. These basic stocks may be used in making all sorts of soups, as well as sauces and stews. Chicken or other poultry stock is especially useful and may be substituted for beef or meat stock if more convenient.

Meat and poultry soups include some of the most beloved and satisfying recipes, evoking childhood memories and the ideals of hearth and home.

Vegetable Beef Soup

This soup is hearty and warming. It's a wonderful way to use fresh garden produce, but frozen vegetables are equally colorful and nutritious. No need to defrost them first.

Serves 6-8

INGREDIENTS

1 lb. stewing steak

14 oz. cans chopped tomatoes in juice

2 onions, finely chopped

2-3 garlic cloves, finely chopped

3 carrots, diced

2 stalks celery, sliced

5½ oz. green cabbage, thinly sliced

1 bay leaf

5-6 allspice berries

¼ tsp. dried thyme

¼ tsp. dried marjoram

4 cups water

4 cups beef stock

7 oz. green beans, cut into short pieces

5½ oz. peas

5½ oz. corn

salt and pepper

1 Trim all visible fat from the steak and cut into ½ inch cubes. Put in a large saucepan with the tomatoes, onions, garlic, carrots, celery, cabbage, bay leaf, allspice, thyme, marjoram, and water.

2 Bring to a boil over a medium-high heat, skimming off any foam that rises to the surface. Stir in the stock, reduce the heat and regulate it so that the soup boils very gently.

Season with salt and pepper. Cook, partially covered, for 1 hour, stirring occasionally.

3 Add the green beans, peas, and corn. Continue cooking for 1 hour longer, or until the meat and vegetables are very tender.

4 Taste and adjust the seasoning, adding salt and pepper as necessary. Ladle into warm bowls and serve.

COOK'S TIP

For quick beef stock, dilute 1 stock cube in 4 cups water, or use a can of beef consommé made up to that quantity with water. Alternatively, you can use all water and add 1 tsp. salt.

Beef Broth with Herbs & Vegetables

This light, lean soup is studded with small diced vegetables and fragrant herbs.
The stock may be used as a basis for other soups.

Serves 4-6

INGREDIENTS

7 oz. celeriac, peeled and finely diced
2 large carrots, finely diced
2 tsp. chopped fresh marjoram leaves
2 tsp. chopped fresh parsley
2 plum tomatoes, skinned, deseeded
   and diced
salt and pepper

BEEF STOCK:
1 lb. 4 oz. boneless beef shin or
   stewing steak, cut into large cubes
1 lb. 10 oz. veal, beef or pork bones
2 onions, quartered
10 cups water
4 garlic cloves, sliced
2 carrots, sliced

1 large leek, sliced
1 stalk celery, cut into 5 cm/2 inch
   pieces
1 bay leaf
4-5 sprigs fresh thyme, or ¼ tsp.
   dried thyme
salt

1 To make the stock, trim as much fat as possible from the beef and put in a large roasting pan with the bones and onions. Roast in a preheated oven at 375° F for 30–40 minutes until browned, turning once or twice. Transfer the ingredients to a large soup pot or flameproof casserole and discard the fat.

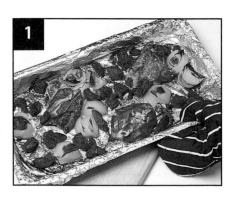

2 Add the water (it should cover by at least 2 inches) and bring to a boil. Skim off any foam that rises to the surface. Reduce the heat and add the sliced garlic, carrots, leek, celery, bay leaf, thyme and a pinch of salt. Simmer very gently, uncovered, for 4 hours, skimming occasionally. Do not stir. If the ingredients emerge from the liquid, top up with water.

3 Gently ladle the stock through a muslin-lined sieve into a large container and remove as much fat as possible. Save the meat for another purpose, if wished, and discard the bones and vegetables. (There should be about 8 cups of stock.)

4 Boil the stock very gently until it is reduced to 6¼ cups, or if the stock already has concentrated flavor, measure out that amount and save the rest for another purpose. Taste the stock and adjust the seasoning if necessary.

5 Bring a saucepan of salted water to a boil and drop in the celeriac and carrots. Reduce the heat, cover and boil gently for about 15 minutes until tender. Drain.

6 Add the herbs to a boiling beef stock. Divide the cooked vegetables and tomatoes among warm bowls, ladle over the boiling stock and serve.

Mexican-style Beef & Rice Soup

For this tasty and unusual soup, boneless leg is a good cut of beef to use,
as it is generally lean and any fat is easily trimmed off.

Serves 4

INGREDIENTS

3 tbsp. olive oil

1 lb. 2 oz. boneless stewing beef, cut into 1 inch pieces

²⁄₃ cup red wine

1 onion, finely chopped

1 green bell pepper, cored, deseeded and finely chopped

1 small fresh red chili, deseeded and finely chopped

2 garlic cloves, finely chopped

1 carrot, finely chopped

¼ tsp. ground coriander

¼ tsp. ground cumin

⅛ tsp. ground cinnamon

¼ tsp. dried oregano

1 bay leaf

grated rind of ½ orange

14 oz. can chopped tomatoes

5 cups beef stock

¼ cup long-grain white rice

3 tbsp. raisins

½ oz. plain semisweet chocolate, melted

chopped fresh cilantro, to garnish

1 Heat half the oil in a large frying pan over a medium-high heat. Add the meat in one layer and cook until well browned, turning to color all sides. Remove the pan from the heat and pour in the wine.

2 Heat the remaining oil in a large saucepan over a medium heat. Add the onion, cover and cook for about 3 minutes, stirring occasionally, until just softened. Add the green bell pepper, chili, garlic, and carrot, and continue cooking, covered, for 3 minutes.

3 Add the coriander, cumin, cinnamon, oregano, bay leaf, and orange rind. Stir in the tomatoes and stock, along with the beef and wine. Bring almost to a boil and when the mixture begins to bubble, reduce the heat to low.

Cover and simmer gently, stirring occasionally, for about 1 hour until the meat is tender.

4 Stir in the rice, raisins, and chocolate, and continue cooking, stirring occasionally, for about 30 minutes until the rice is tender.

5 Ladle into warm bowls and garnish with cilantro.

Beef Goulash Soup

This aromatic dish originates from Hungary, where goulash soups are often served with dumplings.
Noodles are a tasty and quick alternative.

Serves 6

INGREDIENTS

1 tbsp. oil

1 lb. 2 oz. lean ground beef

2 onions, finely chopped

2 garlic cloves, finely chopped

2 tbsp. all-purpose flour

1 cup water

14 oz. can chopped tomatoes in juice

1 carrot, finely chopped

8 oz. red bell pepper, roasted, peeled, deseeded, and chopped

1 tsp. Hungarian paprika

¼ tsp. caraway seeds

pinch of dried oregano

4 cups beef stock

2 oz. tagliatelle, broken into small pieces

salt and pepper

sour cream and cilantro to garnish

1 Heat the oil in a large wide saucepan over a medium-high heat. Add the beef and sprinkle with salt and pepper. Fry until lightly browned.

2 Reduce the heat and add the onions and garlic. Cook for about 3 minutes, stirring frequently, until the onions are softened. Stir in the flour and continue cooking for 1 minute.

3 Add the water and stir to combine well, scraping the bottom of the pan to mix in the flour. Stir in the tomatoes, carrot, pepper, paprika, caraway seeds, oregano, and stock.

4 Bring just to a boil. Reduce the heat, cover and simmer gently for about 40 minutes, stirring occasionally, until all the vegetables are tender.

5 Add the noodles to the soup and simmer for an additional 20 minutes, or until the noodles are cooked.

6 Taste the soup and adjust the seasoning, if necessary. Ladle into warm bowls and top each with a tablespoonful of sour cream. Garnish with cilantro.

Lemon Veal Soup
with Mushrooms

Delicately scented with lemon, this luscious soup features the classic combination of tender veal with mushrooms and cream. Use white mushrooms to retain the light color.

Serves 4

INGREDIENTS

12 oz. boneless veal, cut into ½ inch
  pieces
4 cups chicken stock
l onion, quartered
2 carrots, thinly sliced
2 garlic cloves, halved
1 pared strip lemon rind

1 bay leaf
1 tbsp. butter
12 oz. small button mushrooms,
  quartered
4 tbsp. cornstarch
½ cup heavy cream
freshly grated nutmeg

fresh lemon juice, to taste (optional)
1-2 tbsp. chopped fresh parsley
salt and pepper

1 Put the veal in a large saucepan and add the stock. Bring just to a boil and skim off any foam that rises to the surface.

2 Add the onion, carrots, garlic, lemon rind, and bay leaf. Season with salt and pepper. Reduce the heat and simmer, partially covered, for about 45 minutes, stirring occasionally, until the veal is very tender.

3 Remove the veal and carrots with a slotted spoon and reserve, covered. Strain the stock into a clean saucepan. Discard the onion and garlic, lemon rind and bay leaf.

4 Melt the butter in a frying pan over a medium-high heat. Add the mushrooms, season, and fry gently until lightly golden. Reserve with the veal and carrots.

5 Mix together the cornstarch and cream. Bring the cooking liquid just to a boil and whisk in the cream mixture. Boil very gently for 2-3 minutes until it thickens, whisking almost constantly.

6 Add the reserved meat and vegetables to the soup and simmer over a low heat for about 5 minutes until heated through. Taste and adjust the seasoning, adding nutmeg and a squeeze of lemon juice, if wished. Stir in the parsley, then ladle into warm bowls and serve.

Cabbage Soup with Sausage

Spicy or smoky sausages add substance to this soup, which makes a hearty and warming supper, served with crusty bread and green salad.

Serves 6

INGREDIENTS

12 oz. lean sausages, preferably
  highly seasoned
2 tsp. oil
1 onion, finely chopped
1 leek, halved lengthwise and thinly
  sliced

2 carrots, halved and thinly sliced
14 oz. can chopped tomatoes
12 oz. young green cabbage, cored
  and coarsely shredded
1-2 garlic cloves, finely chopped
pinch dried thyme

6¼ cups chicken or meat stock
salt and pepper
freshly grated Parmesan cheese, to
  serve

1 Put the sausages in water to cover generously and bring to a boil. Reduce the heat and simmer until firm. Drain the sausages and, when cool enough to handle, remove the skin, if you wish, and slice thinly.

2 Heat the oil in a large saucepan over a medium heat, add the onion, leek and carrots and cook for 3–4 minutes, stirring frequently, until the onion starts to soften.

3 Add the tomatoes, cabbage, garlic, thyme, stock, and sausages. Bring to a boil, reduce the heat to low and cook gently, partially covered, for about 40 minutes until the vegetables are tender.

4 Taste the soup and adjust the seasoning, if necessary. Ladle into warm bowls and serve with Parmesan cheese.

VARIATION

If you don't have fresh stock available, use water instead, with 1 stock cube only dissolved in it. Add a little more onion and garlic, plus a bouquet garni (remove it before serving).

Pork Chili Soup

This meaty chili tastes lighter than one made with beef.
Good for informal entertaining, the recipe is easily doubled.

Serves 3

INGREDIENTS

2 tsp. olive oil
1 lb. 2 oz. lean ground pork
1 onion, finely chopped
1 stalk celery, finely chopped
1 bell pepper, cored, deseeded and
   finely chopped
2–3 garlic cloves, finely chopped

3 tbsp. tomato paste
14 oz. can chopped tomatoes in juice
2 cups chicken or meat stock
⅛ tsp. ground coriander
⅛ tsp. ground cumin
¼ tsp. dried oregano
1 tsp. mild chili powder, or to taste

salt and pepper
chopped fresh cilantro or parsley, to
   garnish
sour cream, to serve

1 Heat the oil in a large saucepan over a medium-high heat. Add the pork, season with salt and pepper, and cook until no longer pink, stirring frequently. Reduce the heat to medium and add the onion, celery, bell pepper, and garlic. Cover and continue cooking for 5 minutes, stirring occasionally, until the onion is softened.

2 Add the tomatoes, tomato paste, and the stock. Add the coriander, cumin, oregano, and chili powder. Stir the ingredients in to combine well.

3 Bring just to a boil, reduce the heat to low, cover and simmer for 30–40 minutes until all the vegetables are very tender. Taste and adjust the seasoning, adding more chili powder if you like it hotter.

4 Ladle the chili into warm bowls and sprinkle with cilantro or parsley. Pass the sour cream separately, or top each serving with a spoonful.

COOK'S TIP

For a festive presentation, pass additional accompaniments, such as grated cheese, chopped scallion and guacamole.

Oriental Pork Meatballs
& Greens in Broth

Steaming the meatballs over the soup gives added flavor to the broth. A bamboo steamer that rests on the top of a saucepan is useful for this recipe.

Serves 6

INGREDIENTS

8 cups chicken stock
3 oz. shiitake mushrooms, thinly
  sliced
6 oz. bok choi or other Oriental
  greens, sliced into thin ribbons
6 scallions, finely sliced
salt and pepper

PORK BALLS:
8 oz. lean ground pork
1 oz. fresh spinach leaves, finely
  chopped
2 scallions, finely chopped
1 garlic clove, very finely chopped
pinch of Oriental 5-spice powder

1 tsp. soy sauce

1 To make the pork balls, put the pork, spinach, scallions, and garlic in a bowl. Add the 5-spice powder and soy sauce and mix until combined.

2 Shape the pork mixture into 24 meatballs. Place them in one layer in a steamer that will fit over the top of a saucepan.

3 Bring the stock just to a boil in a saucepan that will accommodate the steamer. Regulate the heat so that the liquid bubbles gently. Add the mushrooms to the stock and place the steamer, covered, on top of the pan. Steam for 10 minutes. Remove the steamer and set aside on a plate.

4 Add the bok choi and scallions to the pan and cook gently in the stock for 3-4 minutes, or until the leaves are wilted. Taste the soup and adjust the seasoning, if necessary.

5 Divide the pork meatballs evenly among 6 warm bowls and ladle the soup over them. Serve at once.

Spicy Lamb Soup with Chickpeas & Zucchini

This thick and hearty main course soup is bursting with exotic flavors and aromas.

Serves 4–5

INGREDIENTS

1-2 tbsp. olive oil

1 lb. lean boneless lamb, such as shoulder or neck fillet, trimmed of fat and cut into ½ inch cubes

1 onion, finely chopped

2-3 garlic cloves, crushed

5 cups water

14 oz. can chopped tomatoes in juice

1 bay leaf

½ tsp. dried thyme

½ tsp. dried oregano

⅛ tsp. ground cinnamon

¼ tsp. ground cumin

¼ tsp. ground turmeric

1 tsp. harissa, or more to taste

14 oz. can chickpeas, rinsed and drained

1 carrot, diced

1 potato, diced

1 zucchini, quartered lengthwise and sliced

3½ oz. fresh or defrosted frozen green peas

chopped fresh mint or cilantro, to garnish

1 Heat the oil in a large saucepan or cast-iron casserole over a medium-high heat. Add the lamb, in batches if necessary to avoid crowding the pan, and cook until evenly browned on all sides, adding a little more oil if needed. Remove the meat, with a slotted spoon, when browned.

2 Reduce the heat and add the onion and garlic to the pan. Cook, stirring frequently, for 1–2 minutes.

3 Add the water and return all the meat to the pan. Bring just to a boil and skim off any foam that rises to the surface. Reduce the heat and stir in the tomatoes, bay leaf, thyme, oregano, cinnamon, cumin, turmeric, and harissa. Simmer for about 1 hour, or until the meat is very tender. Discard the bay leaf.

4 Stir in the chickpeas, carrot and potato and simmer for 15 minutes. Add the zucchini and peas and continue simmering for 15–20 minutes, or until all the vegetables are tender.

5 Adjust the seasoning, adding more harissa, if desired. Ladle the soup into warm bowls, garnish with mint or cilantro.

Scotch Broth

This traditional winter soup is full of goodness,
with lots of tasty golden vegetables along with tender barley and lamb.

Serves 4-6

INGREDIENTS

⅓ cup pearl barley

10½ oz. lean boneless lamb, such as
　shoulder or neck fillet, trimmed of
　fat and cut into ½ inch cubes

3 cups water

1 onion, finely chopped

2 garlic cloves, finely chopped or
　crushed

4 cups chicken or meat stock1 bay
　leaf

1 large leek, quartered lengthwise and
　sliced

2 large carrots, finely diced

1 parsnip, finely diced

4½ oz. peeled rutabaga, diced

2 tbsp. chopped fresh parsley

salt and pepper

1 Rinse the barley under cold running water. Put in a saucepan and cover generously with water. Bring to a boil and boil for 3 minutes, skimming off the foam from the surface. Set aside, covered, in the saucepan.

2 Put the lamb in a large saucepan with the water and bring to a boil. Skim off the foam that rises to the surface.

3 Stir in the garlic, stock, onion, and bay leaf. Reduce the heat and boil very gently, partially covered, for 15 minutes.

4 Drain the barley and add to the soup. Add the leek, carrots, parsnip, and rutabaga. Continue simmering for about 1 hour, or until the lamb and vegetables are tender, stirring occasionally.

5 Taste and adjust the seasoning. Stir in the parsley and ladle into warm bowls to serve.

COOK'S TIP

This soup is lean when the lamb is trimmed. By making it beforehand, you can remove any hardened fat before reheating.

Asian Lamb Soup

This soup needs a light stock. If using a stock cube, make it up to half strength, as it will gain flavor from the vegetables and herbs.

Serves 4

INGREDIENTS

5½ oz. lean tender lamb, such as neck fillet or leg steak

2 garlic cloves, very finely chopped

2 tbsp. soy sauce

5 cups chicken stock

1 tbsp. grated peeled fresh ginger

2 inch piece lemon grass, sliced into very thin rounds

¼ tsp. chili paste, or to taste

6-8 cherry tomatoes, quartered

4 scallions, sliced finely

1¾ oz. bean sprouts, snapped in half

2 tbsp. cilantro leaves

1 tsp. olive oil

1 Trim all visible fat from the lamb and slice the meat thinly. Cut the slices into bite-sized pieces. Spread the meat in one layer on a plate and sprinkle over the garlic and 1 tbsp. of the soy sauce. Leave to marinate, covered, for at least 10 minutes or up to 1 hour.

2 Put the stock in a saucepan with the ginger, lemon grass, remaining soy sauce, and the chili paste. Bring just to a boil, reduce the heat, cover and simmer for

10-15 minutes. Warm 4 ovenproof bowls in a low oven.

3 When ready to serve the soup, drop the tomatoes, scallions, bean sprouts, and cilantro leaves into the stock.

4 Heat the oil in a frying pan and add the lamb with its marinade. Stir-fry the lamb just until it is no longer red and divide among the warm bowls.

5 Ladle over the hot stock and serve immediately.

VARIATION

Substitute lean, tender pork or beef instead of lamb. If preferred, use spinach or Chinese basil, sliced into thin ribbons, in place of cilantro leaves.

Chicken Soup with Stars

How delicious a simple, fresh soup can be. Chicken wings are good to use for making the stock, as the meat is very sweet and doesn't dry out.

Serves 5–6

INGREDIENTS

2¾ oz. small pasta stars, or other very small shapes
chopped fresh parsley

CHICKEN STOCK:
2 lb. 8 oz. chicken pieces, such as wings or legs

10 cups water
1 celery stalk, sliced
1 large carrot, sliced
1 onion, sliced
1 leek, sliced
2 garlic cloves, crushed
8 peppercorns

4 allspice berries
3–4 parsley stems
2–3 fresh thyme sprigs
1 bay leaf
½ tsp. salt
pepper

1 Put the chicken in a large 16 cup pot with the water, celery, carrot, onion, leek, garlic, peppercorns, allspice, herbs, and salt. Bring just to a boil and skim off the foam that rises to the surface. Reduce the heat and simmer, partially covered, for 2 hours.

2 Remove the chicken from the stock and set aside to cool. Continue simmering the stock, uncovered, for about 30 minutes.

When the chicken is cool enough to handle, remove the meat from the bones and, if necessary, cut into bite-sized pieces.

3 Strain the stock and remove as much fat as possible. Discard the vegetables and flavorings. (There should be about 7½ cups of chicken stock.)

4 Bring the stock to a boil in a clean saucepan. Add the pasta and regulate the heat so that the

stock boils very gently. Cook for about 10 minutes, or until the pasta is tender.

5 Stir in the chicken meat. Taste the soup and adjust the seasoning. Ladle into warm bowls and serve sprinkled with parsley.

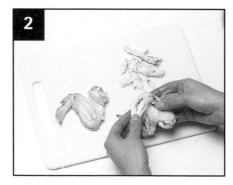

Chicken Broth
with Cheese Noodles

*These homemade noodles require no special equipment. They are tasty and simple
to make. A flavorful stock is essential, but meat stock would be equally good.*

Serves 4

INGREDIENTS

1 egg yolk
⅓ cup freshly grated Parmesan cheese
2 tbsp. all-purpose flour
freshly grated nutmeg
1 tsp. water, or as needed

5 cups chicken stock
1 tbsp. shredded basil leaves or
  chopped tarragon leaves
2 tsp. finely chopped fresh parsley
salt and pepper

freshly grated Parmesan cheese,
  to serve

1 Combine the egg yolk,
Parmesan cheese, and flour
in a mixing bowl. Add a grating of
nutmeg, a pinch of salt and plenty
of freshly ground pepper.

2 Add the water and stir with a
fork until the dough comes
together and pulls away from the
sides of the bowl. (It should be
very stiff.) If the dough is too
crumbly, add more water by half
teaspoons. If the dough is too
sticky, add more flour by

teaspoons until it holds together
and does not stick to your hands.

3 Cut the dough in quarters.
Working with one quarter at a
time, roll the dough into a sausage
shape until it exceeds the width of
your two hands. Break in half and
roll into thin strings, ⅛ inch in
diameter or less (as thin as
possible); break into shorter
lengths as needed. Lay the strings
on a cutting board, well spaced.
Repeat with the remaining dough.

Leave to dry for 15–45 minutes
and cut into 1 inch lengths.

4 Put the stock in a large
saucepan and bring to a boil.
Reduce the heat and regulate it so
the liquid bubbles gently. Taste
and season with salt and pepper.
Drop in the noodles and cook for
5–6 minutes until they are tender.
Stir in the shredded basil and
chopped parsley. Ladle into warm
bowls and serve with freshly
grated Parmesan cheese.

Chicken & Rice Soup

Any kind of rice is suitable for this soup—white or brown long-grain rice,
or even wild rice. Leftover cooked rice is a handy addition for soups.

Serves 4

INGREDIENTS

6¼ cups chicken stock (see Cook's Tip)
2 small carrots, very thinly sliced
1 stalk celery, finely diced
1 baby leek, halved lengthwise and
 thinly sliced

4 oz. tiny peas, defrosted if frozen
1 cup cooked rice
5½ oz. cooked chicken meat, sliced
2 tsp. chopped fresh tarragon
1 tbsp. chopped fresh parsley

salt and pepper
fresh parsley sprigs, to garnish

1 Put the stock in a large saucepan and add the carrots, celery, and leek. Bring to a boil, reduce the heat to low and simmer gently, partially covered, for 10 minutes.

2 Stir in the peas, rice, and chicken meat and continue cooking for an additional 10–15 minutes, or until the vegetables are tender.

3 Add the chopped tarragon and parsley, then taste and adjust the seasoning, adding salt and pepper as needed.

4 Ladle the soup into warm bowls, garnish with parsley and serve.

VARIATIONS

If a baby leek is not available, use 2 scallions instead. If you wish, add a handful of spinach or sorrel leaves, cut into thin ribbons, with these herbs.

COOK'S TIP

If the stock you are using is a little weak, or if you have used a stock cube, add the herbs at the beginning, so that they can flavor the stock for a longer time.

Cream of Chicken & Asparagus

This delectable soup is best made with fairly large asparagus with long stems.
Short-stemmed asparagus will give less flavor to the creamy soup base.

Serves 4

INGREDIENTS

12 oz. asparagus

2 tsp. butter

1 onion, halved and sliced

1 leek, sliced

4 tbsp. white rice

4 cups chicken stock

1 bay leaf

²/₃ cup heavy cream

6 oz. cooked chicken, cut into thin
slices

salt and pepper

1 Remove and discard woody bases of the asparagus. Using a vegetable peeler, peel the asparagus stems. Cut off the tips and set aside. Chop the stems into small pieces.

2 Bring a small saucepan of salted water to a boil and drop in the asparagus tips. Cook for 1–2 minutes until bright green and barely tender. If they are large, slice in half lengthwise. Reserve the asparagus tips.

3 Heat the butter in a large saucepan over a medium heat and add the onion and leek. Cover and cook for 3–4 minutes, stirring frequently, until the onion is soft.

4 Add the asparagus stems, rice, stock and bay leaf with a pinch of salt. Bring just to a boil, reduce the heat, cover and simmer for 30–35 minutes or until the rice and vegetables are very soft. Remove the bay leaf.

5 Allow the soup to cool slightly, then transfer to a blender or food processor and purée until smooth, working in batches if necessary. (If using a food processor, strain off the cooking liquid and reserve. Purée the soup solids with enough cooking liquid to moisten them, then combine with the remaining liquid.)

6 Return the soup to the saucepan and place over a medium-low heat. Stir in the chicken and reserved asparagus tips, then the cream. Taste and adjust the seasoning, adding salt, if needed, and pepper. Simmer for 5–10 minutes until heated through, stirring occasionally. Ladle the soup into warm bowls and serve.

Chicken, Corn, & Bean Soup

This soup is especially tasty using fresh corn kernels cut from 3 or 4 ears of corn. However, frozen corn is a quick and easy alternative.

Serves 6

INGREDIENTS

1 ½ tbsp. butter
1 large onion, finely chopped
1 garlic clove, finely chopped
3 tbsp. all-purpose flour
2½ cups water
4 cups chicken stock

1 carrot, quartered and thinly sliced
6 oz. green beans, trimmed and cut into short pieces
14 oz. can lima beans, drained and rinsed
12 oz. cooked corn or frozen corn

kernels
8 oz. cooked chicken meat
salt and pepper

1 Melt the butter in a large saucepan over a medium-low heat. Add the onion and garlic and cook, stirring frequently, for 3–4 minutes until just softened.

2 Stir in the flour and continue cooking for 2 minutes, stirring occasionally.

3 Gradually pour in the water, stirring constantly and scraping the bottom of the pan to mix in the flour. Bring to a boil, stirring frequently, and cook for 2 minutes. Add the stock and stir until smooth.

4 Add the carrot, green beans, butter beans, corn, and chicken meat. Season with salt and pepper. Bring back to a boil, reduce the heat to medium-low, cover and simmer for about 35 minutes until the vegetables are tender.

5 Taste the soup and adjust the seasoning, adding salt, if needed, and plenty of pepper.

6 Ladle the soup into warm, deep bowls and serve.

VARIATIONS

Replace the lima beans with 10½ oz. cooked fresh broad beans, peeled if wished, or lima beans. You could also substitute sliced runner beans for the green beans.

Chicken, Leek, & Celery Soup

This gently flavored pale green soup is well balanced and very satisfying.
It is suitable either for a starter or light lunch.

Serves 3–4

INGREDIENTS

4 cups chicken stock
1 bay leaf
7 oz. skinless boned chicken breast
4 tbsp. all-purpose flour
2 tsp. butter

1 small onion, finely chopped
3 large leeks, including green parts, thinly sliced
2 stalks celery, peeled and thinly sliced

2 tbsp. heavy cream
freshly grated nutmeg
salt and pepper
fresh cilantro or parsley, to garnish

1 Heat the stock in a small saucepan with the bay leaf until it is steaming. Add the chicken breast and simmer gently for 20 minutes, or until firm to the touch. Discard the bay leaf. Remove the chicken and, when cool enough to handle, cut into small cubes.

2 Put the flour in a bowl. Very slowly whisk in enough of the stock to make a smooth liquid, adding about half the chicken stock.

3 Heat the butter in a heavy-based saucepan over a medium-low heat. Add the onion, leeks, and half of the celery. Cook for about 5 minutes, stirring frequently, until the leeks begin to soften.

4 Slowly pour in the flour and stock mixture and bring to a boil, stirring constantly. Stir in the remaining stock, with a large pinch of salt if it is unsalted. Reduce the heat, cover and cook gently for about 25 minutes until the vegetables are tender.

5 Allow the soup to cool slightly, then transfer to a blender or food processor and purée until smooth, working in batches, if necessary. (If using a food processor, strain off the cooking liquid and reserve for later. Purée the soup solids with enough cooking liquid to moisten them, then combine with the remaining liquid.)

6 Return the soup to the saucepan and stir in the cream and nutmeg. Season with salt, if needed, and pepper. Place over a medium-low heat. Add the chicken breast and remaining celery to the soup. Simmer for about 15 minutes, until the celery is just tender, stirring occasionally. Taste and adjust the seasoning, ladle into warm bowls and sprinkle with cilantro or parsley.

Senegalese Soup

This delicately curried chicken soup requires a flavorful stock.
Its velvety texture makes it an elegant starter.

Serves 4

INGREDIENTS

5 cups chicken stock
1 small onion, thinly sliced
1 small carrot, finely chopped
1 stalk celery, finely chopped
½ small apple, peeled, cored, and
   chopped

1–2 garlic cloves, halved
1 tsp. mild curry powder
7 oz. skinless, boneless chicken breast
2 egg yolks
4 tbsp. cornstarch
1 cup whipping cream

freshly grated nutmeg
salt and white pepper
toasted coconut strips or pecans, to
   garnish

1 Heat the stock in a large saucepan. Add the onion, carrot, celery, apple, garlic, and curry powder with a large pinch of salt, if the stock is unsalted. Bring to a boil, reduce the heat and simmer, covered, for 20 minutes.

2 Trim any fat from the chicken. Add the chicken to the stock and continue simmering for 10 minutes, or until the chicken is tender. Remove the chicken with a slotted spoon.

3 Strain the stock and discard the stock vegetables. Spoon off any fat. When cool enough to handle, cut the chicken into thin slivers.

4 Put the strained stock in a large heavy-based saucepan and put over a medium heat. When starting to bubble around the edge, adjust the heat so it continues to bubble gently at the edge but remains still in the centre.

5 Put the egg yolks in a bowl. Add the cornstarch and cream and whisk until smooth. Whisk one quarter of the hot stock into the cream mixture, then pour it all back into the saucepan, whisking constantly. With a wooden spoon, stir constantly for 10 minutes until the soup thickens slightly. Do not allow it to boil or the soup may curdle. If you see the soup beginning to boil, take the pan off the heat and stir more quickly until it cools down.

6 Stir in the chicken and reduce the heat to low. Season the soup with salt, pepper, and nutmeg. Ladle into warm soup bowls, garnish with toasted coconut strips or pecans and serve.

Chicken Gumbo Soup

*This soup contains okra, an essential ingredient in a gumbo. It helps thicken the soup,
which starts with the traditional Cajun base of cooked flour and oil.*

Serves 6

INGREDIENTS

2 tbsp. olive oil

4 tbsp. all-purpose flour

1 onion, finely chopped

1 small green bell pepper, cored,
   deseeded and finely chopped

1 stalk celery, finely chopped

5 cups chicken stock

14 oz. can chopped tomatoes in juice

3 garlic cloves, finely chopped or
   crushed

4½ oz. okra, stems removed, cut into
   ¼ inch thick slices

4 tbsp. white rice

7 oz. cooked chicken, cubed

4 oz. cooked garlic sausage, sliced or
   cubed

1 Heat the oil in a large heavy-
based saucepan over a
medium-low heat and stir in the
flour. Cook for about 15 minutes,
stirring occasionally, until the
mixture is a rich golden brown
(see Cook's Tip).

2 Add the onion, green bell
pepper, and celery and
continue cooking for about 10
minutes until the onion softens.

3 Slowly pour in the stock and
bring to a boil, stirring well

and scraping the bottom of the
pan to mix in the flour. Remove
the pan from the heat.

4 Add the tomatoes and garlic.
Stir in the okra and rice and
season. Reduce the heat, cover and
simmer for 20 minutes, or until
the okra is tender.

6 Add the chicken and sausage
and continue simmering for
about 10 minutes. Taste and adjust
the seasoning, if necessary, and
ladle into warm bowls to serve.

COOK'S TIP

*Keep a watchful eye on the roux
(flour and oil) as it begins to
darken. The soup gains a lot of
flavor from this traditional Cajun
base, but if it burns the soup will be
bitter. If you prefer, omit it and start
by cooking the onion, green bell
pepper, and celery in the oil, adding
the flour when they are softened.*

Thai-style Chicken & Coconut Soup

Make this soup when you want a change from traditional chicken soup.
It is nicely spicy. Use a generous amount of fresh cilantro to garnish.

Serves 4

INGREDIENTS

5 cups chicken stock

7 oz. skinless boned chicken

1 fresh chili, split lengthwise and
  deseeded

3 inch piece lemon grass, split
  lengthwise

3-4 lime leaves

1 inch piece fresh ginger, peeled and
  sliced

½ cup coconut milk

6-8 scallions, sliced diagonally

¼ tsp. chili paste, or to taste

salt

fresh cilantro, to garnish

1 Put the stock in a pan with the chicken, chili, lemon grass, lime leaves, and ginger. Bring almost to a boil, reduce the heat, cover and simmer for 20–25 minutes, or until the chicken is cooked through and firm to the touch.

2 Remove the chicken and strain the stock. When the chicken is cool, slice thinly or shred into bite-sized pieces.

3 Return the stock to the saucepan and heat to simmering. Stir in the coconut milk and scallions. Add the chicken and continue simmering for about 10 minutes, until the soup is heated through and the flavors have mingled.

4 Stir in the chili paste. Season to taste with salt and, if wished, add a little more chili paste.

5 Ladle into warm bowls and float fresh cilantro on top to serve.

COOK'S TIP

Once the stock is flavored and the chicken cooked, this soup is very quick to finish. If you wish, poach the chicken and strain the stock ahead of time. Store in the refrigerator separately.

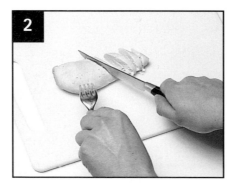

Chicken & Spring Vegetable Soup

This creamy soup is filled with chunky vegetables and aromatic herbs.
Using baby vegetables give the soup an attractive look.

Serves 4

INGREDIENTS

4 cups chicken stock
6 oz. skinless boned chicken breast
fresh parsley and tarragon sprigs
2 garlic cloves, crushed
4½ oz. baby carrots, halved or
    quartered
8 oz. small new potatoes, quartered

4 tbsp. all-purpose flour
½ cup milk
4-5 scallions, sliced diagonally
3 oz. asparagus tips, halved and cut
    into 1½ inch pieces
½ cup whipping or heavy cream
1 tbsp. finely chopped fresh parsley

1 tbsp. finely chopped fresh tarragon
salt and pepper

1 Put the stock in a saucepan with the chicken, parsley and tarragon sprigs and garlic. Bring just to a boil, reduce the heat, cover and simmer for 20 minutes, or until the chicken is cooked through and firm to the touch.

2 Remove the chicken and strain the stock. When the chicken is cool enough to handle, cut into bite-sized pieces.

3 Return the stock to the saucepan and bring to a boil. Adjust the heat so the liquid boils very gently. Add the carrots, cover and cook for 5 minutes. Put in the potatoes, cover again and cook for about 12 minutes, or until the vegetables are beginning to become tender.

4 Meanwhile, put the flour in a small mixing bowl and very slowly whisk in the milk to make a

thick paste. Stir in a little of the hot stock mixture to make a smooth liquid.

5 Stir in the flour mixture and bring just to a boil, stirring. Boil gently for 4-5 minutes until it thickens, stirring frequently.

6 Add the scallions, asparagus, and chicken. Reduce the heat a little and simmer for about 15 minutes, until all the vegetables are tender. Stir in the cream and herbs. Season and serve.

VARIATION

If cooking on a budget or preparing a hearty family dish, substitute peas for the asparagus.

Turkey Soup with Rice, Mushrooms, & Sage

This is a warming wintery soup, substantial enough to serve as a main course, with lots of crusty bread.

Serves 4–5

INGREDIENTS

3 tbsp. butter

1 onion, finely chopped

1 stalk celery, finely chopped

25 large fresh sage leaves, finely chopped

4 tbsp. all-purpose flour

5 cups turkey or chicken stock

⅔ cup brown rice

9 oz. mushrooms, sliced

7 oz. cooked turkey

¾ cup heavy cream

freshly grated Parmesan cheese, to serve

1 Melt half the butter in a large saucepan over a medium-low heat. Add the onion, celery, and sage and cook for 3-4 minutes until the onion is softened, stirring frequently. Stir in the flour and continue cooking for 2 minutes.

2 Slowly add about one quarter of the stock and stir well, scraping the bottom of the pan to mix in the flour. Pour in the remaining stock, stirring to combine completely, and bring just to a boil.

3 Stir in the rice and season with salt and pepper. Reduce the heat and simmer gently, partially covered, for about 30 minutes until the rice is just tender, stirring occasionally.

4 Meanwhile, melt the remaining butter in a large frying pan over a medium heat. Add the mushrooms and season with salt and pepper. Cook for about 8 minutes until they are golden brown, stirring occasionally at first, then more often after they start to color. Add the mushrooms to the soup.

5 Add the turkey to the soup and stir in the cream. Continue simmering for about 10 minutes until heated through. Taste and adjust the seasoning, if necessary. Ladle into warm bowls and serve with Parmesan cheese.

Provençal Turkey Soup

No need to wait for Christmas leftovers to make this soup. Prepacked turkey, such as boneless breast or stir-fry meat, makes this a year-round favorite.

Serves 4–5

INGREDIENTS

1 tbsp. olive oil

2 red, yellow or green bell peppers, cored, deseeded and finely chopped

1 stalk celery, thinly sliced

1 large onion, finely chopped

½ cup dry white wine

14 oz. can plum tomatoes in juice

3-4 garlic cloves, finely chopped

4 cups turkey or chicken stock

¼ tsp. dried thyme

1 bay leaf

2 zucchini, finely diced

12 oz. cooked cubed turkey

salt and pepper

fresh basil leaves, to garnish

---

1 Heat the oil in a large saucepan over a medium heat. Add the bell peppers, celery, and onion and cook for about 8 minutes until softened and just beginning to color.

2 Add the wine and bubble for 1 minute. Add the tomatoes and garlic.

3 Stir in the stock. Add the thyme and bay leaf, season with salt and pepper and bring to

a boil. Reduce the heat, cover and simmer for about 25 minutes until the vegetables are tender.

4 Add the zucchini and turkey. Continue cooking for another 10-15 minutes until the zucchini are completely tender.

5 Taste the soup and adjust the seasoning. Ladle into warm bowls, garnish with basil leaves and serve.

COOK'S TIP

A large turkey leg can be used to make this soup. Put in a pan, add water to cover generously, and add one each carrot, celery stalk, leek, and onion, coarsely chopped, and a little salt; poach for 3 hours. Reserve the meat, discard the skin, bone, and vegetables, and remove the fat from the stock before making the soup.

Asian Duck Broth

This soup combines delicate flavors with a satisfying meaty taste.

Serves 4–6

INGREDIENTS

2 duck leg quarters, skinned

4 cups water

2½ cups chicken stock

1 inch piece fresh ginger, peeled and sliced

1 large carrot, sliced

1 onion, sliced

1 leek, sliced

3 garlic cloves, crushed

I tsp. black peppercorns

2 tbsp. soy sauce, or to taste

I small carrot, cut into thin strips or slivers

I small leek, cut into thin strips or

slivers

3½ oz. shiitake mushrooms, thinly sliced

1 oz. watercress leaves

salt and pepper

1 Put the duck in a large saucepan with the water. Bring just to a boil and skim off the foam that rises to the surface. Add the stock, ginger, carrot, onion, leek, garlic, peppercorns, and soy sauce. Reduce the heat and simmer, partially covered, for 1½ hours.

2 Remove the duck from the stock and set aside. When the duck is cool enough to handle, remove the meat from the bones and slice thinly or shred into bite-sized pieces, discarding any fat.

3 Strain the stock and press with the back of a spoon to extract all the liquid. Remove as much fat as possible. Discard the vegetables and herbs.

4 Bring the stock just to a boil in a clean saucepan and add the strips of carrot and leek and the mushrooms together with the duck meat. Reduce the heat and cook gently for 5 minutes, or until the carrot is just tender.

5 Stir in the watercress and continue simmering for 1–2 minutes until it is wilted. Taste the soup and adjust the seasoning if needed, adding a little more soy sauce if wished. Ladle the soup into warm bowls and serve at once.

Hunter's Soup

This soup is perfect for the sweet meat of rabbit, which is traditionally paired with tomatoes and mushrooms. This recipe is also suitable for venison.

Serves 4

INGREDIENTS

1-2 tbsp. olive oil
2 lb. rabbit, jointed
1 onion, finely chopped
2-3 garlic cloves, finely chopped or crushed
3½ oz. lean bacon, finely chopped
½ cup white wine

5 cups chicken stock
2 cups tomato juice
2 tbsp. tomato paste
2 carrots, halved lengthwise and sliced
1 bay leaf
¼ tsp. dried thyme

¼ tsp. dried oregano
1 tbsp. butter
10½ oz. mushrooms, quartered if small or sliced
chopped fresh parsley, to garnish

1 Heat the oil in a large saucepan or flameproof casserole over a medium-high heat. Add the rabbit, in batches if necessary to avoid crowding, and cook until lightly browned on all sides, adding a little more oil if needed. Remove the pieces when browned.

2 Reduce the heat a little and add the onion, garlic, and bacon to the pan. Cook, stirring frequently, for 2 more minutes.

3 Add the wine and bubble for 1 minute. Add the stock and return the rabbit to the pan with any juices. Bring to a boil and skim off any foam that rises to the surface. Reduce the heat and stir in the tomato juice, tomato paste, carrots, bay leaf, thyme, and oregano. Season with salt and pepper. Cover and simmer gently for 1 hour, or until very tender.

4 Remove the rabbit pieces with a slotted spoon and, when cool enough to handle, remove the meat from the bones. Discard any fat or gristle, along with the bones. Cut the meat into bite-sized pieces and return to the soup.

5 Melt the butter in a frying pan over a medium-high heat. Add the mushrooms and season with salt and pepper. Fry gently until lightly golden, then add to the soup. Simmer for 10-15 minutes to blend. Season to taste and serve sprinkled with parsley.

Soups with Beans & Grains

Heartwarming and nourishing soups based on beans, pulses and grains are traditional in many different countries. Soups using these ingredients often stand in for other protein sources as a dietary foundation, yet they can be perfect for light, refined soups as well.

To prepare beans and pulses, first spread them on a plate and pick over to remove any stones or foreign matter. Most benefit from soaking—from about 6 up to 24 hours. Those dried within the year (i.e., this year's crop) need the least soaking. Lentils do not require soaking. Cooking time for beans and pulses varies quite a bit; sometimes they need longer than expected to become tender. Do not add salt until they are cooked, as salt toughens the skins and may prevent them from cooking properly.

Canned beans can be convenient and are best added at a point in a recipe so they are not cooked a long time. Those packed without salt or sugar have the best texture.

Grains such as rice, barley, and oats provide variety in soups, as well as nourishment. These grains may be the main ingredient of a satisfying soup or a pleasing and healthful soup addition. The following recipes demonstrate the versatility of soups based on beans, and grains.

White Bean Soup with Olive Tapenade

*In this elegant soup, the pungent green olive purée provides a pleasant
counterpoint to the natural sweetness of the beans.*

Serves 8

INGREDIENTS

12 oz. dried navy beans

1 tbsp. olive oil

1 large onion, finely chopped

1 large leek (white part only), thinly
sliced

3 garlic cloves, finely chopped

2 stalk celery, finely chopped

2 small carrots, finely chopped

1 small fennel bulb, finely chopped

8 cups water

¼ tsp. dried thyme

¼ tsp. dried marjoram

salt and pepper

TAPENADE:

1 garlic clove

1 small bunch fresh flat-leaf parsley,
stems removed

8½ oz. almond-stuffed green olives,
drained

5 tbsp. olive oil

1 Pick over the beans, cover
generously with cold water
and leave to soak for 6 hours or
overnight. Drain the beans, put in
a saucepan and add cold water to
cover by 2 inches. Bring to the
boil and boil for 10 minutes.
Drain and rinse well.

2 Heat the oil in a large heavy-
based saucepan over a
medium heat. Add the onion and
leek, cover and cook for 3–4
minutes, stirring occasionally,

until just softened. Add the garlic,
celery, carrots, and fennel, and
continue cooking for 2 minutes.

3 Add the water, drained beans
and the herbs. When the
mixture begins to bubble, reduce
the heat to low. Cover and simmer
gently, stirring occasionally, for
about 1½ hours until the beans are
very tender.

4 Meanwhile make the
tapenade. Put the garlic,

parsley, and drained olives in a
blender or food processor with the
olive oil. Blend to a purée and
scrape into a small serving bowl.

5 Allow the soup to cool slightly,
then transfer to a blender or
food processor and purée until
smooth, working in batches if
necessary. (If using a food
processor, strain off the cooking
liquid and reserve. Purée the soup
solids with enough cooking liquid
to moisten them, then combine
with the remaining liquid.)

6 Return the puréed soup to
the saucepan and thin with a
little water, if necessary. Season
with salt and pepper to taste, and
simmer until heated through.
Ladle into warm bowls and serve,
stirring a generous teaspoon of the
tapenade into each serving.

Confetti Bean Soup

This soup uses the colorful dried bean mixes available that include a variety of different beans.
Brightly colored vegetables are added for a lively combination.

Serves 8

INGREDIENTS

1 lb. 2 oz. mixed dried beans
1 tbsp. olive oil
2 onions, finely chopped
1 yellow or orange bell pepper, cored, deseeded and finely chopped
3 garlic cloves, finely chopped or crushed

2 carrots, cubed
1 parsnip, cubed
2 stalks celery, halved lengthwise and cut into ¼ inch pieces
3½ oz. lean smoked ham, cubed
8 cups water
2 tbsp. tomato paste

⅛ tsp. dried thyme
1 bay leaf
1 potato, finely diced
1 tbsp. chopped fresh marjoram
2 tbsp. chopped fresh parsley
salt and pepper

1 Pick over the beans, cover generously with cold water and leave to soak for 6 hours or overnight. Drain the beans, put in a saucepan and add enough cold water to cover by 2 inches. Bring to the boil and boil for 10 minutes, skimming off the foam as it accumulates. Drain and rinse well.

2 Heat the oil in a large saucepan over a medium heat. Add the onions and bell pepper, cover and cook for 3–4 minutes, stirring occasionally, until the onion is just softened. Add the garlic, carrots, parsnip, celery, and ham and continue cooking for 2–3 minutes, or until the onion begins to color.

3 Add the water, drained beans, tomato paste, thyme and bay leaf. Bring just to the boil, cover and simmer, occasionally stirring, for 1¼ hours, or until the beans and vegetables are tender.

4 Put the potato in a small saucepan and ladle over just enough of the bean cooking liquid to cover the potatoes. Bring to the boil, cover the pan, reduce the heat and boil gently for about 12 minutes or until the potato is very tender.

5 Put the potato and its cooking liquid into a blender or food processor, then add 3 ladlefuls of the beans with a small amount of their liquid and purée until completely smooth.

6 Scrape the purée into the saucepan, add the marjoram and parsley and stir to blend. Season the soup to taste, adding salt and pepper generously. Reheat gently over a medium-low heat until hot and ladle the soup into warm bowls.

Minestrone

This winter vegetable soup makes good use of seasonal vegetables. Vary them according to what is available, including rutabaga and winter squash if you wish.

Serves 6–8

INGREDIENTS

1 tbsp. olive oil
1 onion, finely chopped
1 leek, halved lengthwise and thinly sliced
2 garlic cloves, finely chopped
14 oz. can chopped tomatoes in juice
1 carrot, finely diced
1 small turnip, finely diced

1 small potato, finely diced
4½ oz. peeled celeriac, finely diced
9 oz. peeled pumpkin or winter squash flesh, finely diced
3 cups water
4 cups chicken or vegetable stock
14 oz. can cannellini or cranberry beans, drained and rinsed
3½ oz. leafy cabbage, such as cavolo

nero
3 oz. small pasta shapes or broken spaghetti
salt and pepper
freshly grated Parmesan cheese, to serve

1 Heat the oil in a large saucepan over a medium heat. Add the onion, leek, and garlic and cook for 3–4 minutes, stirring occasionally, until slightly softened.

2 Add the tomatoes, carrot, turnip, potato, celeriac, pumpkin, water, and stock. Bring to the boil, stirring occasionally.

3 Stir in the beans and cabbage. Season lightly with salt and pepper. Reduce the heat and simmer, partially covered, for about 50 minutes until all the vegetables are tender.

4 Bring salted water to the boil in a saucepan. Add the pasta and cook until it is just tender. Drain and add to the soup.

5 Taste the soup and adjust the seasoning. Ladle into warm bowls and serve with Parmesan cheese to sprinkle on top.

COOK'S TIP

*The dark leaves of the Italian cabbage, **cavolo nero**, are particularly attractive in this colorful soup.*

Vegetable Chili

This is a hearty and flavorful soup that is good on its own or spooned over cooked rice or baked potatoes for a more substantial meal.

Serves 5–6

INGREDIENTS

1 medium eggplant, peeled if wished, cut into 1 inch slices

1 tbsp. olive oil, plus extra for brushing

1 large red or yellow onion, finely chopped

2 bell peppers, finely chopped

3–4 garlic cloves, finely chopped or crushed

14 oz. cans chopped tomatoes in juice

1 tbsp. mild chili powder, or to taste

½ tsp. ground cumin

½ tsp. dried oregano

2 small zucchini, quartered lengthwise and sliced

14 oz. can kidney beans, drained and rinsed

2 cups water

1 tbsp. tomato paste

6 scallions, finely chopped

4 oz. grated cheddar cheese

salt and pepper

1 Brush the eggplant slices on one side with olive oil. Heat half the oil in a large frying pan over a medium-high heat. Add the eggplant, oiled side up, and cook for 5–6 minutes until browned on one side. Turn, brown the other side and transfer to a plate. Cut into bite-sized pieces.

2 Heat the remaining oil in a large saucepan over a medium heat. Add the onion and bell peppers, cover and cook for 3–4 minutes, stirring occasionally, until the onion is just softened. Add the garlic and continue cooking for 2–3 minutes, or until the onion begins to color.

3 Add the tomatoes, chili powder, cumin, and oregano. Season with salt and pepper. Bring just to the boil, reduce the heat, cover and simmer for 15 minutes.

4 Add the zucchini, eggplant pieces, and beans. Stir in the water and tomato paste. Cover again and continue simmering for about 45 minutes, or until the vegetables are tender. Taste and adjust the seasoning. If you prefer it hotter, stir in a little more chili powder.

5 Season to taste. Ladle into bowls, and top with scallions and cheese.

Beans & Greens Soup

Include some pungent greens in this soup, if you can.
They add a wonderful gutsy flavor, and of course are very good for you!

Serves 4

INGREDIENTS

9 oz. dried navy or cannellini beans
1 tbsp. olive oil
2 onions, finely chopped
4 garlic cloves, finely chopped
1 stalk celery, thinly sliced

2 carrots, halved and thinly sliced
5 cups water
¼ tsp. dried thyme
¼ tsp. dried marjoram
1 bay leaf

4½ oz. leafy greens, such as chard,
  mustard, spinach, and kale, washed
salt and pepper

1 Pick over the beans, cover generously with cold water and leave to soak for 6 hours or overnight. Drain the beans, put in a saucepan and add enough cold water to cover by 2 inches. Bring to the boil and boil for 10 minutes. Drain and rinse well.

2 Heat the oil in a large saucepan over a medium heat. Add the onion and cook, covered, for 3–4 minutes, stirring occasionally, until the onion is just softened. Add the garlic, celery, and carrots, and continue cooking for 2 minutes.

3 Add the water, drained beans, thyme, marjoram, and bay leaf. When the mixture begins to bubble, reduce the heat to low. Cover and simmer gently, stirring occasionally, for about 1¼ hours until the beans are tender; the cooking time will vary depending on the type of bean. Season with salt and pepper.

4 Allow the soup to cool slightly, then transfer 2 cups to a blender or food processor. Purée until smooth and recombine with the soup.

5 A handful at a time, cut the greens crossways into thin ribbons, keeping tender leaves like spinach separate. Add the thicker leaves and cook gently, uncovered, for 10 minutes. Stir in any remaining greens and continue cooking for 5–10 minutes, until all the greens are tender.

6 Taste and adjust the seasoning, if necessary. Ladle the soup into warm bowls and serve.

Greek Bean Soup with Lemon & Mint

This is based on a simple and variable bean soup typical in Greek home cooking. The artichoke hearts make it a bit fancier and more interesting, but they are not essential.

Serves 6

INGREDIENTS

1 tbsp. olive oil
1 large onion, finely chopped
1 large carrot, finely diced
2 stalks celery, finely chopped
4 tomatoes, skinned, deseeded, and chopped, or 9 oz. drained canned tomatoes

2 garlic cloves, finely chopped
14 oz. cans cannellini or haricot beans, drained and rinsed well
5 cups water
1 zucchini, finely diced
grated rind of ½ lemon
1 tbsp. chopped fresh mint, or ¼ tsp.

dried mint
1 tsp. chopped fresh thyme, or ⅛ tsp. dried thyme
1 bay leaf
14 oz. can artichoke hearts
salt and pepper

1 Heat 1 teaspoon of the olive oil in a large saucepan over a medium heat. Add the onion and cook for 3–4 minutes, stirring occasionally, until the onion softens. Add the carrot, celery, tomatoes and garlic and continue cooking for an additional 5 minutes, stirring frequently.

2 Add the beans and water. Bring to the boil, reduce the heat, cover and cook gently for about 10 minutes.

3 Add the zucchini, lemon rind, mint, thyme and bay leaf and season with salt and pepper. Cover and simmer about 40 minutes until all the vegetables are tender. Allow to cool slightly. Transfer 2 cups to a blender or food processor, purée until smooth, and recombine.

4 Meanwhile, heat the remaining oil in a frying pan over a medium heat, adding more if necessary to coat the bottom of the pan. Fry the artichokes, cut side down, until lightly browned. Turn over and fry long enough to heat through.

5 Ladle the soup into warm bowls and top each with an artichoke heart.

Kidney Bean, Pumpkin, & Tomato Soup

Pumpkin, a greatly underrated vegetable, balances the spicy heat in this soup and gives it a splash of color, too.

Serves 4–6

INGREDIENTS

9 oz. dried kidney beans
1 tbsp. olive oil
2 onions, finely chopped
4 garlic cloves, finely chopped
1 stalk celery, thinly sliced
1 carrot, halved and thinly sliced
2 tsp. tomato paste

⅛ tsp. dried thyme
⅛ tsp. dried oregano
⅛ tsp. ground cumin
5 cups water
1 bay leaf
14 oz. can chopped tomatoes in juice
9 oz. peeled pumpkin flesh, diced

¼ tsp. chili paste, or to taste
salt and pepper
fresh cilantro, to garnish

1 Pick over the beans, cover generously with cold water and leave to soak for 6 hours or overnight. Drain the beans, put in a saucepan and add enough cold water to cover by 2 inches. Bring to the boil and boil for 10 minutes. Drain and rinse well.

2 Heat the oil in a large saucepan over a medium heat. Add the onions and cook, covered, for 3–4 minutes until they are just softened, stirring occasionally. Add the garlic, celery, and carrot, and continue cooking for 2 minutes.

3 Add the water, drained beans, tomato paste, thyme, oregano, cumin, water, and bay leaf. When the mixture begins to bubble, reduce the heat to low. Cover and simmer gently for 1 hour, stirring occasionally.

4 Stir in the tomatoes, pumpkin and chili paste and continue simmering for about 1 hour more, or until the beans and pumpkin are tender, stirring from time to time.

5 Taste and season the soup, stir in a little more chili paste if liked. Ladle the soup into bowls, garnish with cilantro and serve.

Split Pea & Ham Soup

A hearty and heartwarming soup, this is perfect for weekend lunches—or make it ahead for a nourishing midweek supper, all ready to reheat.

Serves 6–8

INGREDIENTS

1 lb. 2 oz. split green peas
1 tbsp. olive oil
1 large onion, finely chopped
1 large carrot, finely chopped
1 stalk celery, finely chopped

4 cups chicken or vegetable stock
4 cups water
8 oz. lean smoked ham, finely diced
¼ tsp. dried thyme
¼ tsp. dried marjoram

1 bay leaf
salt and pepper

1 Rinse the peas under cold running water. Put in a saucepan and cover generously with water. Bring to the boil and boil for 3 minutes, skimming off the foam from the surface. Drain the peas.

2 Heat the oil in a large saucepan over a medium heat. Add the onion and cook for 3–4 minutes, stirring occasionally, until just softened.

3 Add the carrot and celery and continue cooking for 2 minutes. Add the peas, pour over the stock and water and stir to combine.

4 Bring just to the boil and stir the ham into the soup. Add the thyme, marjoram, and bay leaf. Reduce the heat, cover and cook gently for 1–1½ hours until the ingredients are very soft. Remove the bay leaf.

5 Taste and adjust the seasoning. Ladle into warm soup bowls and serve.

VARIATION

You could add sliced, cooked sausages instead of or in addition to the ham. If you have a ham bone, use in place of the diced ham. Trim off the fat and cook the bone in the soup. Before serving, remove the bone, cut off the meat and return the meat to the soup.

Split Pea & Parsnip Soup

*This soup is surprisingly delicate. The yellow peas give it an appealing light color,
while the parsnips add an aromatic flavor.*

Serves 4

INGREDIENTS

9 oz. split yellow peas
1 tbsp. olive oil
1 onion, finely chopped
1 small leek, finely chopped
3 garlic cloves, finely chopped

2 parsnips, sliced (about 8 oz.)
8 cups water
10 sage leaves, or ¼ tsp. dried sage
⅛ tsp. dried thyme
¼ tsp. ground coriander

1 bay leaf
salt and pepper
freshly grated nutmeg
chopped fresh cilantro or parsley, to
    garnish

1 Rinse the peas well under cold running water. Put in a saucepan and cover generously with water. Bring to the boil and boil for 3 minutes, skimming off the foam from the surface. Drain the peas.

2 Heat the oil in a large saucepan over a medium heat. Add the onion and leek and cook for about 3 minutes, stirring frequently, until just softened. Add the garlic and parsnips and continue cooking for 2 minutes, stirring occasionally.

3 Add the peas, water, sage, thyme, coriander, and bay leaf. Bring almost to the boil, reduce the heat, cover and cook gently for about 40 minutes until the vegetables are very soft. Remove the bay leaf.

4 Allow the soup to cool slightly, then transfer to a blender or food processor and purée until smooth, working in batches if necessary. (If using a food processor, strain off the cooking liquid and reserve. Purée the soup solids with enough

cooking liquid to moisten them, then combine with the remaining liquid.)

5 Return the soup to the saucepan and thin with a little more water, if wished. Season generously with salt, pepper, and nutmeg. Place over a low heat and simmer until reheated. Ladle into warm soup plates and garnish with fresh cilantro or parsley.

Chickpea Soup with Kale & Chorizo

This soup is satisfying and colorful, with an appealing piquancy from the chorizo. Try to find the Iberico style, which is more meaty and lean.

Serves 4

INGREDIENTS

9 oz. dried chickpeas, soaked overnight in cold water to cover generously

4½ oz. lean chorizo, peeled and finely diced

1 onion, finely chopped

1 shallot, finely chopped

1 carrot, thinly sliced

2 garlic cloves, finely chopped

14 oz. can chopped tomatoes in juice

5 cups water

1 bay leaf

¼ tsp. dried thyme

¼ tsp. dried oregano

8 oz. pumpkin, diced

8 oz. potato, diced

4½ oz. curly kale leaves, finely chopped

salt and pepper

1 Drain the chickpeas and put in a saucepan with enough cold water to cover generously. Bring to the boil over a high heat and cook for 10 minutes. Drain.

2 Put the chorizo in a large saucepan over a medium-low heat. Cook for 5–10 minutes, stirring, frequently to render as much fat as possible. Remove with a slotted spoon and drain on paper towels.

3 Pour off the fat and add the onion, shallot, carrot and garlic. Cook for 3–4 minutes.

4 Add the chickpeas, tomatoes, water, herbs, and chorizo. Bring almost to the boil, reduce the heat, cover and cook gently for 30 minutes.

5 Stir in the pumpkin and potato, cover and continue cooking for about 30 minutes until the chickpeas are tender. Season with salt and pepper.

6 Stir in the kale and continue to cook, uncovered, for 15–20 minutes, or until it is tender. Taste and adjust the seasoning. Ladle into warm bowls and serve.

COOK'S TIP

You can easily chop the kale in a food processor; it should be like chopped parsley. Alternatively, slice crosswise into very thin ribbons.

Spicy Potato & Chickpea Soup

This soup uses ingredients you are likely to have on hand, yet it is far from standard fare.
Spicy and substantial, it makes a delicious meal-in-a-bowl, ideal for a midweek supper.

Serves 4

INGREDIENTS

1 tbsp. olive oil

1 large onion, finely chopped

2–3 garlic cloves, finely chopped or
   crushed

1 carrot, quartered and thinly sliced

12 oz. potatoes, diced

¼ tsp. ground turmeric

¼ tsp. garam masala

¼ tsp. mild curry powder

14 oz. can chopped tomatoes
   in juice

3¾ cups water

14 oz. can chopped tomatoes in juice

¼ tsp. chili paste, or to taste

14 oz. can chickpeas, rinsed and
   drained

3 oz. fresh or frozen peas

salt and pepper

chopped fresh cilantro, to garnish

1 Heat the olive oil in a large saucepan over a medium heat. Add the onion and garlic and cook for 3–4 minutes, stirring occasionally, until the onion is beginning to soften.

2 Add the carrot, potatoes, turmeric, garam masala and curry powder and continue cooking for 1–2 minutes.

3 Add the tomatoes, water, and chili paste with a large pinch of salt. Reduce the heat, cover and simmer for 30 minutes, stirring occasionally.

4 Add the chickpeas and peas to the pan, continue cooking for about 15 minutes, or until all the vegetables are tender.

5 Taste the soup and adjust the seasoning, if necessary, adding a little more chili if wished. Ladle into warm soup bowls and sprinkle with cilantro.

Hummus & Zucchini Soup

*This light and elegant soup couldn't be easier. Its subtle flavor makes it
a great starter for entertaining, especially when feeding vegetarians.*

Serves 4

INGREDIENTS

1 tsp. olive oil	2 cups vegetable or chicken stock	finely chopped fresh parsley, to
1 small onion	6 oz. ready-made hummus	garnish
3 zucchini, sliced	fresh lemon juice, to taste	
(about 1 lb.)	salt and pepper	

1 Heat the oil in a saucepan over a medium heat. Add the onion and zucchini, cover and cook for about 3 minutes, stirring occasionally, until they begin to soften.

2 Add the stock and season lightly with salt and pepper. Bring to the boil, reduce the heat, cover and cook gently for about 20 minutes until the vegetables are tender.

3 Allow the soup to cool slightly, then transfer to a blender or food processor and purée until smooth. (If using a food processor, strain off the cooking liquid and reserve. Purée the soup solids with enough cooking liquid to moisten them, then combine with the remaining liquid.)

4 Add the hummus to the puréed soup in the blender or processor and process to combine.

5 Return the soup to the saucepan and reheat gently over a medium-low heat. Taste and adjust the seasoning, adding a little lemon juice if wished. Ladle into warm bowls, sprinkle with parsley and serve.

COOK'S TIP

If you wish peel the zucchini. It gives the soup a nice pale color.

VARIATION

This soup is also delicious served cold chill—well before serving.

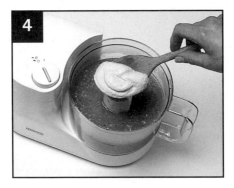

Tomato & Lentil Soup

This soup is simple and satisfying, with subtle, slightly exotic flavors.
It uses ingredients you are likely to have on hand, so it's ideal for a last-minute meal.

Serves 6

INGREDIENTS

1 tbsp. olive oil	9 oz. split red lentils	1 bay leaf
1 leek, thinly sliced	5 cups water	salt and pepper
1 large carrot, quartered and thinly sliced	1½ cups tomato juice	chopped fresh dill or parsley, to garnish
1 large onion, finely chopped	14 oz. can chopped tomatoes in juice	
2 garlic cloves, finely chopped	¼ tsp. ground cumin	
	¼ tsp. ground coriander	

1 Heat the oil in a large saucepan over a medium heat. Add the leek, carrot, onion, and garlic. Cover and cook for 4–5 minutes, stirring frequently, until the leek and onion are slightly softened.

2 Rinse and drain the lentils (check for any small stones). Add the lentils to the pan and stir in the water, tomato juice, and tomatoes. Add the cumin, coriander, and bay leaf with a large pinch of salt. Bring to the boil, reduce the heat and simmer for about 45 minutes, or until the vegetables are tender.

3 If you prefer a smooth soup, allow it to cool slightly, then transfer to a blender or food processor and purée until smooth, working in batches if necessary. (If using a food processor, strain off the cooking liquid and reserve. Purée the soup solids with enough cooking liquid to moisten them, then combine with the remaining liquid.) Only purée about half of the soup, if you prefer a more chunky soup.

4 Return the puréed soup to the saucepan and stir to blend. Season with salt and pepper to taste. Simmer over a medium-low heat until reheated.

5 Ladle the soup into warm bowls, garnish with dill or parsley and serve.

Curried Lentil Soup with Fried Onion Garnish

This soup is a typical Indian treatment of lentils, called dhal. Often dhals are served as a thick purée, but in this version the consistency is slightly thinner to make it easier for spooning.

Serves 4–6

INGREDIENTS

2 tsp. olive oil

1 large onion, finely chopped

1 large leek, thinly sliced

1 large carrot, grated

1–2 garlic cloves, finely chopped

½ tsp. chili paste

½ tsp. grated peeled fresh ginger or
   ginger paste

½ tsp. garam masala or curry powder

¼ tsp. ground cumin

⅛ tsp. ground turmeric

5 cups water

9 oz. split red lentils or yellow split
   peas

salt and pepper

TO GARNISH:

1 red onion, halved and thinly sliced
   into half-rings

oil, for frying

1 Heat the olive oil in a large saucepan over a medium heat. Add the onion and cook for 4–5 minutes, stirring frequently, until it just begins to brown. Add the leek, carrot and garlic and continue cooking for 2 minutes, stirring occasionally.

2 Stir in the chili paste, ginger, garam masala, or curry

powder, cumin, and turmeric. Add the water and stir to mix well.

3 Rinse and drain the lentils (check for any small stones). Add to the saucepan. Bring to the boil, reduce the heat, cover and simmer gently for 35 minutes, or until the lentils and vegetables are very soft, stirring occasionally.

4 Allow the soup to cool slightly, then transfer to a blender or food processor and purée until smooth, working in batches if necessary. (If using a food processor, strain off the cooking liquid and reserve. Purée the soup solids with enough cooking liquid to moisten them, then combine with the remaining liquid.)

5 Return the soup to the saucepan and simmer over a low heat. Season with salt and pepper to taste.

6 For the fried onion garnish, heat oil to a depth of about ½ inch in a small frying pan over a medium-high heat until it begins to smoke. Drop in about one-third of the onion slices and fry until deep golden brown. Using a slotted spoon, transfer to paper towels and drain. Cook the remainder of the onion slices in batches and drain.

7 Ladle the soup into warm bowls and scatter the fried onions over the top. Serve the soup immediately.

Green Lentil, Potato, & Ham Soup

A comforting and satisfying cold-weather soup, this is good served with bread as a light main course, but not too filling to be a starter soup, served in smaller portions.

Serves 5–6

INGREDIENTS

10½ oz. Puy lentils
2 tsp. butter
1 large onion, finely chopped
2 carrots, finely chopped
1 garlic clove, finely chopped
2 cups water

1 bay leaf
¼ tsp. dried sage or rosemary
8 oz. potatoes, diced
  (see Cook's Tip)
4 cups chicken stock
1 tbsp. tomato paste

4 oz. smoked ham, finely diced
salt and pepper
chopped fresh parsley, to garnish

1 Rinse and drain the lentils and check for any small stones.

2 Melt the butter in a large saucepan or flameproof casserole over a medium heat. Add the onion, carrots, and garlic, cover and cook for 4–5 minutes until the onion is slightly softened, stirring frequently.

3 Add the lentils to the vegetables with the water, bay leaf, and sage or rosemary. Bring to the boil, reduce the heat, cover and simmer for 10 minutes.

4 Add the stock, potatoes, tomato paste, and ham. Bring back to a simmer. Cover and continue simmering for 25–30 minutes, or until the vegetables are tender.

5 Season to taste with salt and pepper and remove the bay leaf. Ladle into warm bowls, garnish with parsley and serve.

COOK'S TIP

Cut the potatoes into small dice, about ¼ inch, so they will be in proportion with the lentils.

Golden Vegetable Soup with Green Lentils

In this simple-to-make soup, the flavors meld after blending to create a delicious taste. It is also very healthy and looks appealing.

Serves 6

INGREDIENTS

1 tbsp. olive oil
1 onion, finely chopped
1 garlic clove, finely chopped
1 carrot, halved and thinly sliced
1 lb. young green cabbage, cored,
   quartered and thinly sliced

14 oz. can chopped tomatoes
   in juice
½ tsp. dried thyme
2 bay leaves
6¼ cups chicken or vegetable stock
7 oz. Puy lentils

2 cups water
salt and pepper
fresh cilantro or parsley, to garnish

1 Heat the oil in a large saucepan over a medium heat, add the onion, garlic and carrot and cook for 3–4 minutes, stirring frequently, until the onion starts to soften. Add the cabbage and cook for an additional 2 minutes.

2 Add the tomatoes, thyme, and 1 bay leaf, then pour in the stock. Bring to the boil, reduce the heat to low and cook gently, partially covered, for about 45 minutes until the vegetables are tender.

3 Meanwhile, put the lentils in another saucepan with the remaining bay leaf and the water. Bring just to the boil, reduce the heat and simmer for about 25 minutes until tender. Drain off any remaining water, and set aside.

4 When the vegetable soup is cooked, allow it to cool slightly, then transfer to a blender or food processor and purée until smooth, working in batches, if necessary. (If using a food processor, strain off the cooking liquid and reserve. Purée the soup solids with enough cooking liquid to moisten them, then combine with the remaining liquid.)

5 Return the soup to the saucepan and add the cooked lentils. Taste and adjust the seasoning, and cook for about 10 minutes to heat through. Ladle into warm bowls and garnish with cilantro or parsley.

Mushroom & Barley Soup

This old-fashioned soup is nourishing and warming, with distinctive flavors and a nice texture. For the best results, use homemade stock.

Serves 4

INGREDIENTS

⅓ cup pearl barley
6¼ cups chicken or vegetable stock
1 bay leaf
1 tbsp. butter

12 oz. mushrooms, thinly sliced
1 tsp. olive oil
1 onion, finely chopped
2 carrots, thinly sliced

1 tbsp. chopped fresh tarragon
1 tbsp. chopped fresh parsley or
tarragon, to garnish

1 Rinse the barley and drain. Bring 2 cups of the stock to the boil in a small saucepan. Add the bay leaf and, if the stock is unsalted, add a large pinch of salt. Stir in the barley, reduce the heat, cover and simmer for 40 minutes.

2 Melt the butter in a large frying pan over a medium heat. Add the mushrooms and season with salt and pepper. Cook for about 8 minutes until they are golden brown, stirring occasionally at first, then more often after they start to color. Remove the mushrooms

from the heat.

3 Heat the oil in a large saucepan over a medium heat and add the onion and carrots. Cover and cook for about 3 minutes, stirring frequently, until the onion is softened.

4 Add the remaining stock and bring to the boil. Stir in the barley with its cooking liquid and add the mushrooms. Reduce the heat, cover and simmer gently for about 20 minutes, or until the carrots are tender, stirring occasionally.

5 Stir in the tarragon and parsley. Taste and adjust the seasoning, if necessary. Ladle into warm bowls, garnish with fresh parsley or tarragon and serve.

COOK'S TIP

The barley will continue to absorb liquid if the soup is stored, so if making ahead, you may need to add a little more stock or water when reheating.

Barley, Fennel, & Broccoli Soup

This rustic vegetable soup is appealing in its simplicity. Served with ciabatta, focaccia, or garlic bread, it makes a good light lunch.

Serves 4

INGREDIENTS

2 oz. pearl barley
6¼ cups chicken or vegetable stock
1 bay leaf
½ tsp. chopped fresh thyme leaves, or
⅛ tsp. dried thyme
9 oz. broccoli head

2 tsp. olive oil
1 large leek, halved lengthwise and
finely chopped
2 garlic cloves, finely chopped
1 stalk celery, thinly sliced
1 large fennel bulb, thinly sliced

1 tbsp. chopped fresh basil
freshly grated Parmesan cheese,
to serve

1 Rinse the barley and drain. Bring 2 cups of the stock to the boil in a small saucepan. Add the bay leaf and thyme. If the stock is unsalted, add a large pinch of salt. Stir in the barley, reduce the heat, partially cover and simmer for 30–40 minutes until tender.

2 Cut the florets off the broccoli head and peel the stem. Cut the stem into very thin matchsticks, about 1 inch long, along with any large stems from the florets. Cut the florets into small slivers and reserve them seperately.

3 Heat the oil in a large pan over a medium-low heat and add the leek and garlic. Cover and cook for about 5 minutes, stirring frequently, until softened. Add the celery, fennel, and broccoli stems and cook for 2 minutes.

4 Stir in the remaining stock and bring to the boil. Add the barley with its cooking liquid.

Season with salt and pepper. Reduce the heat, cover and simmer gently for 10 minutes, stirring occasionally.

5 Uncover the pan and adjust the heat so the soup bubbles gently. Stir in the broccoli florets and continue cooking for 10–12 minutes, or until the broccoli is tender. Stir in the basil. Taste and adjust the seasoning, if necessary. Ladle into warm bowls and serve with plenty of Parmesan cheese to sprinkle over.

Rice & Black-eyed Pea Soup

*This soup is satisfying and very healthy. Brown rice gives a pleasing chewy texture,
but white rice could be used instead.*

Serves 4–6

INGREDIENTS

9 oz. dried black-eyed peas
1 tbsp. olive oil
1 large onion, finely chopped
2 garlic cloves, finely chopped or
  crushed
2 carrots, finely chopped
2 stalks celery, finely chopped

1 small red bell pepper, deseeded and
  finely chopped
3 oz. lean smoked ham,
  finely diced
½ tsp. fresh thyme leaves, or ⅛ tsp.
  dried thyme
1 bay leaf

5 cups chicken or vegetable stock
2½ cups water
½ cup brown rice
chopped fresh parsley or chives, to
  garnish

1 Pick over the beans, cover generously with cold water and leave to soak for at least 6 hours or overnight. Drain the beans, put in a saucepan and add enough cold water to cover by 5 cm/2 inches. Bring to the boil and boil for 10 minutes. Drain and rinse well.

2 Heat the oil in a large heavy-based saucepan over a medium heat. Add the onion, cover and cook for 3–4 minutes, stirring frequently, until just softened. Add the garlic, carrots, celery, and bell pepper, stir well and cook for an additional 2 minutes.

3 Add the drained beans, ham, thyme, bay leaf, stock, and water. Bring to the boil, reduce the heat, cover and simmer gently, stirring occasionally, for 1 hour, or until the beans are just tender.

4 Stir in the rice and season the soup with salt, if needed, and pepper. Continue cooking for 30 minutes, or until the rice and beans are tender.

5 Taste the soup and adjust the seasoning, if necessary. Ladle into warm bowls and serve garnished with parsley or chives.

Wild Rice & Spinach Soup

Although it is generally classed as a grain, wild rice is actually a native North American grass that grows in water. It adds a delicious texture to this soup.

Serves 4

INGREDIENTS

2 tsp. olive oil

3 oz. smoked Canadian bacon, finely chopped

1 large onion, finely chopped

⅔ cup wild rice, rinsed in cold water and drained

5 cups water

1–2 garlic cloves, finely chopped or crushed

1 bay leaf

½ cup all-purpose flour

2 cups milk

8 oz. spinach leaves, finely chopped

1 cup heavy cream

freshly grated nutmeg

salt and pepper

1 Heat the oil in a large saucepan over a medium heat. Add the bacon and cook for 6–7 minutes until lightly browned. Add the onion and wild rice and continue cooking for 3–4 minutes, stirring frequently, until the onion softens.

2 Add the water, garlic, and bay leaf and season with a little salt and pepper. Bring to the boil, reduce the heat, cover and boil very gently for about 1 hour, or until some of the grains of wild rice have split open.

3 Put the flour in a mixing bowl and very slowly whisk in enough of the milk to make a thick paste. Add the remainder of the milk, whisking to make a smooth liquid. Put the flour and milk mixture in a saucepan and ladle in as much of the rice cooking liquid as possible. Bring to the boil, stirring almost constantly. Reduce the heat so that the liquid just bubbles gently and cook for 10 minutes, stirring occasionally. Add the spinach and cook for 1–2 minutes until wilted.

4 Allow the soup to cool slightly, then transfer to a blender or food processor and purée, working in batches if necessary. (If using a food processor, strain off the cooking liquid and reserve. Purée the soup solids with enough cooking liquid to moisten them, then combine with the remaining liquid.)

5 Combine the puréed soup with the rice mixture in a saucepan and place over a medium-low heat. Stir in the cream and a grating of nutmeg. Simmer the soup until reheated. Taste and adjust the seasoning, if needed, and ladle into warm bowls.

Tomato & Rice Soup

*This is a good soup for impromptu entertaining,
especially if you have leftover rice on hand.*

Serves 4

INGREDIENTS

1 tbsp. olive oil

1 large onion, finely chopped

2 garlic cloves, finely chopped or
    crushed

2 carrots, grated

1 stalk celery, thinly sliced

14 oz. cans plum tomatoes in juice

1 tsp. dark brown sugar, or to taste

3¾ cups vegetable stock or water

1 bay leaf

1 cup cooked white rice

2 tbsp. chopped fresh dill

6 tbsp. heavy cream

salt and pepper

fresh dill sprigs, to garnish

1 Heat the olive oil in a large saucepan over a medium heat. Add the onion, cover and cook for 3–4 minutes, stirring occasionally, until the onion is just softened.

2 Add the garlic, carrots, celery, tomatoes, brown sugar, and stock or water with the bay leaf to the saucepan. Reduce the heat, cover and simmer for 1 hour, stirring occasionally.

3 Allow the soup to cool slightly, then transfer to a blender or food processor and purée until smooth, working in batches if necessary. (If using a food processor, strain off the cooking liquid and reserve. Purée the soup solids with enough cooking liquid to moisten them, then combine with the remaining liquid.)

4 Return the soup to the saucepan and stir in the rice

and dill. Season with salt, if needed, and pepper. Cook gently over a medium-low heat for about 5 minutes, or until hot.

5 Stir in the cream. Taste the soup and adjust the seasoning, if necessary. Ladle into warm soup bowls and garnish each serving with a swirl of cream and dill sprigs. Serve at once.

Vegetable Soup with Bulgur & Herbs

This healthy and colorful soup makes good use of your herb garden.
The fresh herbs give it a vibrant flavor.

Serves 5–6

INGREDIENTS

1 tbsp. olive oil

2 onions, chopped

3 garlic cloves, finely chopped or crushed

⅓ cup bulgur wheat

5 tomatoes, skinned and sliced, or 14 oz. can plum tomatoes in juice

8 oz. peeled pumpkin or acorn squash, diced

1 large zucchini, quartered lengthwise and sliced

4 cups boiling water

2 tbsp. tomato paste

¼ tsp. chili paste

1½ oz. chopped mixed fresh oregano, basil and flat-leaf parsley

1 oz. arugula leaves, coarsely chopped

1⅓ cups shelled fresh or frozen peas

salt and pepper

freshly grated Parmesan cheese, to serve

1 Heat the oil in a large saucepan over a medium-low heat and add the onions and garlic. Cover and cook for 5–8 minutes until the onions soften.

2 Stir in the bulgur wheat and continue cooking for 1 minute.

3 Layer the tomatoes, pumpkin, or squash and zucchini in the saucepan.

4 Combine half the water with the tomato paste, chili paste, and a large pinch of salt. Pour over the vegetables. Cover and simmer for 15 minutes.

5 Uncover the saucepan and stir. Put all the herbs and the arugula on top of the soup and layer the peas over them. Pour over the remaining water and gently bring to the boil. Reduce the heat and simmer for about 20–25 minutes, or until all the vegetables are tender.

6 Stir the soup. Taste and adjust the seasoning, adding salt and pepper if necessary, and a little more chili paste if you wish. Ladle into warm bowls and serve with Parmesan cheese.

Piquant Oatmeal Soup

This unusual soup, of Mexican origin, is simple and comforting.
It has a hint of chili heat, but its character is more sweet than spicy.

Serves 6

INGREDIENTS

1 cup rolled oats

3 tbsp. butter

1 large sweet onion

2–3 garlic cloves

12 oz. tomatoes, skinned, deseeded

and chopped

6 cups chicken stock

⅛ tsp. ground cumin

1 tsp. harissa, or ½ tsp. chili paste

1–2 tbsp. lime juice

salt and pepper

chopped scallions, to garnish

1 Place a heavy-based frying pan over a medium heat. Add the oats and toast for about 25 minutes, stirring frequently, until lightly and evenly browned. Remove the oats from the pan and allow to cool.

2 Heat the butter in a large saucepan over a medium heat. Add the onion and garlic and cook until the onion is softened.

3 Add the tomatoes, stock, cumin, harissa, or chili paste and a good pinch of salt to the softened onion and garlic.

4 Stir in the oats and bring to the boil. Regulate the heat so that the soup boils gently and cook for 6 minutes.

5 Stir in 1 tablespoon of the lime juice. Taste and adjust the seasoning. Add more lime juice if desired. Ladle the soup into warm bowls and sprinkle with scallions, to garnish.

COOK'S TIP

This soup is very quick to prepare once the oats are toasted. The oats could be prepared in advance at a convenient time.

VARIATIONS

Substitute lemon juice for the lime juice, using a little less.

Special Occasion & Cold Soups

The selection of soups in this chapter offers something a little different. Special occasion soups are particularly appropriate for entertaining, either because of their festive ingredients or their suitability for an informal gathering, or perhaps because they require more preparation time than a family supper normally allows. The cold soups are also great for special occasions and home entertaining, but may be equally welcome on a hot summer's day.

Cold soups require advance preparation so they have time to chill, but most of these soups can be prepared ahead to some extent. As a general rule, reheat soup slowly over low to medium-low heat just until it is hot throughout and steaming. If cream is added at the end, wait and add this when reheating.

When entertaining, provide an array of choices particulalry suited to entertaining. Think about what is in season and how you like to entertain friends and family and look at this chapter for inspiration.

Lobster Bisque

This rich and elegant starter soup is perfect for a special dinner. The lobster shell, made into a stock, contributes greatly to the flavor of the soup.

Serves 4

INGREDIENTS

1 lb. cooked lobster
3 tbsp. butter
1 small carrot, grated
1 stalk celery, finely chopped
1 leek, finely chopped
1 small onion, finely chopped

2 shallots, finely chopped
3 tbsp. brandy or Cognac
¼ cup dry white wine
5 cups water
1 tbsp. tomato paste
½ cup whipping cream, or to taste

6 tbsp. all-purpose flour
salt and pepper
snipped fresh chives, to garnish

1 Pull off the lobster tail. With the legs up, cut the body in half lengthwise. Scoop out the tomalley (the soft pale greenish-gray part) and, if it is a female, the roe (the solid red-orange part). Reserve these together, covered and refrigerated. Remove the meat and cut into bite-sized pieces; cover and refrigerate. Chop the shell into large pieces.

2 Melt half the butter in a large saucepan over a medium heat and add the lobster shell pieces.

Fry until brown bits begin to stick on the bottom of the pan. Add the carrot, celery, leek, onion, and shallots. Cook, stirring, for 1½–2 minutes (do not let it burn). Add the alcohol and bubble for 1 minute. Pour over the water, add the tomato paste, a large pinch of salt and bring to a boil. Reduce the heat, simmer for 30 minutes and strain the stock, discarding the solids.

3 Melt the remaining butter in a small saucepan and add the

tomalley and roe, if any. Add the cream, whisk to mix well, remove from the heat and set aside.

4 Put the flour in a small mixing bowl and very slowly whisk in 2–3 tablespoons of cold water. Stir in a little of the hot stock mixture to make a smooth liquid.

5 Bring the remaining lobster stock to a boil and whisk in the flour mixture. Boil gently for 4–5 minutes until the soup thickens, stirring frequently. Press the tomalley, roe and cream mixture through a sieve into the soup. Reduce the heat and add the reserved lobster meat. Simmer gently until heated through.

6 Taste the soup and adjust the seasoning, adding more cream if desired. Ladle into warm bowls, sprinkle with chives and serve.

Creamy Oyster Soup

This soup makes a rich and elegant starter. Serve it in shallow bowls so the oysters are visible, and make sure you warm the bowls to keep the soup hot.

Serves 4

INGREDIENTS

12 oysters
2 tbsp. butter
2 shallots, finely chopped
5 tbsp. white wine

1¼ cups fish stock
¾ cup whipping or heavy cream
2 tbsp. cornstarch, dissolved in 2 tbsp.
cold water

salt and pepper
caviar or lumpfish roe, to garnish
(optional)

1 To open the oysters, hold flat-side up, over a sieve set over a bowl to catch the juices, and push an oyster knife into the hinge. Work it around until you can pry off the top shell. When all the oysters have been opened, strain the liquid through a sieve lined with damp muslin. Remove any bits of shell stuck to the oysters and reserve them in their liquid.

2 Melt half the butter in a saucepan over a low heat. Add the shallots and cook gently for about 5 minutes until just softened, stirring frequently; do not allow them to brown.

3 Add the wine, bring to a boil and boil for 1 minute. Stir in the fish stock, bring back to a boil and boil for 3–4 minutes. Reduce the heat to a gentle simmer.

4 Add the oysters and their liquid and poach for about 1 minute until they become more firm but are still tender. Remove the oysters with a slotted spoon and reserve, covered. Strain the stock.

5 Bring the strained stock to a boil in a clean saucepan. Add the cream and bring back to a boil.

6 Stir the dissolved cornstarch into the soup and boil gently for 2–3 minutes, stirring frequently, until slightly thickened. Add the oysters and cook for 1–2 minutes to reheat them. Taste and adjust the seasoning, if necessary, and ladle the soup into warm bowls. Top each serving with a teaspoon of caviar or roe, if using.

Bouillabaisse

*This soup makes a festive seafood extravaganza
worthy of a special celebration.*

Serves 6

INGREDIENTS

1 lb. jumbo shrimp
1 lb. 10 oz. lb. firm white fish fillets,
    such as sea bass, snapper, and
    monkfish
4 tbsp. olive oil
grated rind of 1 orange
1 large garlic clove, finely chopped
½ tsp. chili paste or harissa
1 large leek, sliced
1 onion, halved and sliced

1 red bell pepper, cored, deseeded,
    and sliced
3–4 tomatoes, cored and cut into
    eighths
4 garlic cloves, sliced
1 bay leaf
pinch of saffron threads
½ tsp. fennel seeds
2½ cups water
5 cups fish stock

1 fennel bulb, finely chopped
1 large onion, finely chopped
8 oz. potatoes, peeled, halved and
    thinly sliced
9 oz. scallops
salt and pepper
toasted French bread slices, to serve
ready-prepared aioli (garlic
    mayonnaise), to serve

1 Peel the shrimp and reserve the shells. Cut the fish fillets into serving pieces about 2 inches square. Trim off any ragged edges and reserve. Put the fish in a bowl with 2 tablespoons of the olive oil, the orange rind, crushed garlic, and chili paste or harissa. Turn to coat well, cover and chill the shrimp and fish separately.

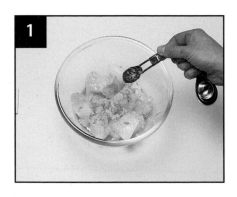

2 Heat 1 tablespoon of the olive oil in a large saucepan over a medium heat. Add the leek, sliced onion and red bell pepper. Cover and cook for about 5 minutes, stirring frequently, until the onion softens. Stir in the tomatoes, sliced garlic, bay leaf, saffron, fennel seeds, shrimp shells, water, and fish stock. Bring to a boil, reduce the heat and simmer, covered, for 30 minutes. Strain the stock, pressing with the back of a spoon to extract all the liquid.

3 To finish the soup, heat the remaining olive oil in a large saucepan. Add the fennel and finely chopped onion and cook for 4–5 minutes until the onion softens, stirring frequently. Add

the stock and potatoes and bring to a boil. Reduce the heat slightly, cover and cook for 12–15 minutes, or until the potatoes are just tender.

4 Adjust the heat so the soup simmers gently and add the fish, starting with any thicker pieces and putting in the thinner ones after 2 or 3 minutes. Add the shrimp and scallops and continue simmering gently until all the seafood is cooked and opaque throughout.

5 Taste the soup and adjust the seasoning. Ladle into warm bowls. Spread the garlic sauce on the toasted bread slices and arrange on top of the soup.

Cioppino

This tomato-based California soup is brimming with seafood, which can be varied according to availability. Serve it with olive bread or ciabatta.

Serves 4–6

INGREDIENTS

1 lb. 2 oz. mussels

1 lb. 2 oz. clams, rinsed

1¼ cups dry white wine

1 tbsp. olive oil

1 large onion, finely chopped

1 stalk celery, finely chopped

1 yellow or green bell pepper, cored, deseeded and finely chopped

14 oz. can chopped tomatoes in juice

3 garlic cloves, very finely chopped

1 tbsp. tomato paste

1 bay leaf

1½ cups fish stock or water

6 oz. small squid, cleaned and cut into small pieces

8 oz. skinless white fish fillets, such as cod, sole, or haddock

5½ oz. small scallops, or cooked shelled shrimp

chopped fresh parsley, to garnish

---

1 Discard any broken mussels and those with open shells that do not close when tapped. Rinse, pull off any "beards," and if there are barnacles, scrape them with a knife under cold running water. Put the mussels in a large heavy-based saucepan. Cover tightly and cook over a high heat for about 4 minutes, or until the mussels open, shaking the pan occasionally.

2 When cool enough to handle, remove the mussels from the shells, adding any additional juices to the cooking liquid. Strain the cooking liquid through a muslin-lined sieve and reserve.

3 Put the clams into a heavy saucepan with ¼ cup of the wine. Cover tightly, place over a medium-high heat and cook for 2–4 minutes, or until they open. Remove the clams from the shells and strain the cooking liquid through a muslin-lined sieve and reserve.

4 Heat the olive oil in a large saucepan over a medium-low heat. Add the onion, celery and bell pepper and cook for 3–4 minutes, until the onion softens, stirring occasionally. Add the remaining wine, tomatoes, garlic, tomato paste, and bay leaf. Continue cooking for 10 minutes.

5 Stir in the fish stock or water, squid and reserved mussel and clam cooking liquids. Bring to a boil, reduce the heat and simmer for 35–40 minutes until the vegetables and squid are tender.

6 Add the fish, mussels, and clams and simmer, stirring occasionally, for about 4 minutes until the fish becomes opaque. Stir in the scallops or shrimp and continue simmering for 3–4 minutes until heated through. Remove the bay leaf, ladle into warm bowls, and sprinkle with chopped parsley.

Black Bean & Sausage Tureen

The Mexican-style garnishes make this a festive dish for informal entertaining.
Include some smoky or spicy sausages for added flavor.

Serves 6–8

INGREDIENTS

3²⁄₃ cups dried black beans
1 tbsp. olive oil
2 onions, finely chopped
4 garlic cloves, finely chopped
8 cups water
14 oz. cans plum tomatoes in juice
1 tbsp. tomato paste
1 bay leaf

½ tsp. ground cumin
¼ tsp. dried oregano
½ tsp. chili paste
1 lb. 9 oz. lean sausages
salt and pepper

TO GARNISH:
2–3 ripe avocados

3–4 tbsp. lime juice
3 tomatoes, skinned, deseeded, and
   chopped
about 1¼ cups sour cream
1 bunch scallions, finely chopped
1 large bunch cilantro, chopped

1 Pick over the beans, cover generously with cold water and leave to soak for 6 hours or overnight. Drain the beans, put in a saucepan and add enough cold water to cover by 2 inches. Bring to a boil and boil for 10 minutes. Drain and rinse well.

2 Heat the oil in a very large pot or flameproof casserole over a medium heat. Add the onions and cook for about 5 minutes, stirring frequently, until they start to color. Add the garlic and continue cooking for 1 minute.

3 Add the water, tomatoes, tomato paste and drained beans. When the mixture begins to bubble, reduce the heat to low. Add the bay leaf, cumin, oregano, and chili paste and stir to mix well. Cover and simmer gently for 1½–2 hours, stirring occasionally, until the beans are very tender. Season with salt and, if needed, pepper.

4 Meanwhile, bake the sausages in a preheated oven at 350˚ F for 40–45 minutes, turning 2 or 3 times for even browning. Drain, slice and add to the beans after they have been cooking for about 1 hour.

5 Peel and dice the avocado. Mix with the lime juice in a bowl and turn to coat. Put all the other garnishes in separate bowls.

6 When the beans are tender, taste the soup and adjust the seasoning. Ladle the soup into warm bowls. Serve with garnishes.

Poached Beef
& Spring Vegetable Soup

This lean, pretty soup makes an elegant light main course for 4, or it will serve 6 as a starter.
A bit of last minute assembly is needed, but it's worth it.

Serves 4–6

INGREDIENTS

12 small new potatoes, quartered

4 slim carrots, quartered lengthwise
and cut into 1½ inch lengths

5½ oz. slender green beans, cut into
1½ inch lengths

6 cups rich beef or meat stock

2 tbsp. soy sauce

3 tbsp. dry sherry

12 oz. beef tenderloin, about 2 inches
thick

5½ oz. shiitake mushrooms, sliced

1 tbsp. chopped fresh parsley

1 tbsp. chopped fresh chives

salt and pepper

1 Bring a saucepan of salted water to a boil and drop in the potatoes and carrots. Reduce the heat, cover and boil gently for about 15 minutes until tender. Bring another saucepan of salted water to a boil, drop in the beans and boil for about 5 minutes until just tender. Drain the vegetables and reserve.

2 Bring the stock to a boil in a saucepan and add the soy sauce and sherry. Season with salt and pepper to taste. Reduce the heat and adjust so that the stock bubbles very gently around the edges. Add the beef and simmer for 10 minutes. (The beef should be very rare, as it will continue cooking in the bowls.)

3 Add the mushrooms and continue simmering for 3 minutes. Warm the bowls in a low oven.

4 Remove the meat from the stock and leave to rest on a carving board. Taste the stock and adjust the seasoning, if necessary. Bring the stock back to a boil.

5 Cut the meat in half lengthwise and slice each half into pieces about ⅛ inch thick. Season the meat lightly with salt and pepper and divide among the warm bowls.

6 Drop the reserved vegetables into the stock and heat through for about 1 minute. Ladle the stock over the meat, dividing the vegetables as evenly as possible. Sprinkle over the herbs and serve.

Chicken & Mushroom Soup with a Puff Pastry Top

This soup needs a rich, flavorful stock, and mushrooms that contribute plenty of flavor. The pastry top is baked separately to simplify serving.

Serves 6

INGREDIENTS

5½ cups stock
4 skinless boned chicken breasts
2 garlic cloves, crushed
small bunch of fresh tarragon or
  ¼ tsp. dried tarragon

1 tbsp. butter
14 oz. chestnut or porcini
  mushrooms, sliced
3 tbsp. dry white wine
6 tbsp. all-purpose flour

¾ cup whipping or heavy cream
13½ oz. puff pastry
2 tbsp. finely chopped fresh parsley
salt and pepper

1 Put the stock in a saucepan and bring just to a boil. Add the chicken, garlic, and tarragon, reduce the heat, cover and simmer for 20 minutes, or until the chicken is cooked through. Remove the chicken and strain the stock. When the chicken is cool, cut into bite-sized pieces.

2 Melt the butter in a large frying pan over a medium heat. Add the mushrooms and season with salt and pepper. Cook for 5–8 minutes until they are golden brown, stirring occasionally at first, then stirring more often after they start to color. Add the wine and bubble briefly. Remove the mushrooms from the heat.

3 Put the flour in a small mixing bowl and very slowly whisk in the cream to make a thick paste. Stir in a little of the stock to make a smooth liquid.

4 Bring the stock to a boil in a large saucepan. Whisk in the flour mixture and bring back to a boil. Boil gently for 3–4 minutes until the soup thickens, stirring frequently. Add the mushrooms and liquid, if any. Reduce the heat to low and simmer very gently, just to keep warm.

5 Cut out 6 rounds of pastry smaller in diameter than the soup bowls, using a plate as a guide. Put on a baking sheet, prick with a fork and bake in a preheated oven at 400° F for about 15 minutes, or until deep golden.

6 Meanwhile, add the chicken meat to the soup. Taste and adjust the seasoning. Simmer for about 10 minutes until the soup is heated through. Stir in the parsley. Ladle the soup into warm bowls and place the pastry rounds on top. Serve immediately.

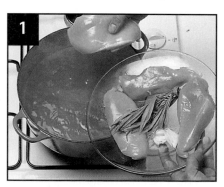

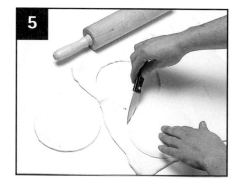

Chicken & Chickpea with Fruit

This main-course soup is Mexican in origin. Its appeal comes from an unusual combination of fruits and vegetables which include sweet, salty, and sour flavors.

Serves 8

INGREDIENTS

1 lb. 12 oz. chicken legs or thighs, skinned
1 stalk celery, sliced
1 large carrot, halved and sliced
1 large onion, finely chopped
2 garlic cloves, finely chopped
10 cups chicken stock
4–5 parsley stems
1 bay leaf

4½ oz. lean smoked ham, diced
14 oz. can chickpeas, drained and rinsed
1 large turnip, diced
2 zucchini, halved and sliced
1 large potato, diced
1 sweet potato, diced
6 oz. corn kernels
3 large pears, peeled, cored and cut

into bite-sized pieces
3 tbsp. fresh lime juice, or to taste
2 tbsp. olive oil
2 very green, unripe bananas, cut into ¼ inch slices
salt and pepper
chopped fresh parsley, to garnish

1 Put the chicken into a large 2 quart saucepan with the celery, carrot, onion, garlic, stock, parsley stems, and bay leaf. Bring just to a boil over a medium-high heat and skim off any foam that rises to the surface. Reduce the heat and simmer, partially covered, for about 45 minutes, or until the chicken is tender.

2 Remove the chicken from the stock. When it is cool, remove the meat from the bones, cut into bite-sized pieces and reserve. Skim the fat as from the stock. Discard the parsley stems and bay leaf.

3 Bring the stock just to the boil. Add the ham, chickpeas, turnip, zucchini, potato, sweet

potato, and corn. Return the meat to the stock. Adjust the heat so the soup simmers gently and cook, partially covered, for about 30 minutes, or until all the vegetables are tender.

4 Add the pears and lime juice to the soup and continue cooking for about 5 minutes, just until they are barely poached. Season to taste, add more lime juice if desired.

5 Heat the oil in a frying pan over a medium-high heat. Fry the bananas until golden. Drain on paper towels and keep warm. Ladle the soup into bowls and top with fried banana slices.

Chicken Ravioli in Tarragon Broth

Making filled pasta requires a bit of time and effort but the results are worth it.
Homemade stock is essential; reduce it to concentrate the flavor if it is weak.

Serves 6

INGREDIENTS

8 cups chicken stock
2 tbsp. finely chopped fresh
 tarragon leaves

HOMEMADE PASTA:
1 cup all-purpose flour, plus extra if
 needed

2 tbsp. fresh tarragon leaves, with
 stems removed
1 egg
1 egg, separated
1 tsp. extra-virgin olive oil
2–3 tbsp. water
FILLING:

7 oz. cooked chicken, coarsely
 chopped
½ tsp. grated lemon rind
2 tbsp. chopped mixed fresh tarragon,
 chives and parsley
4 tbsp. whipping cream
salt and pepper

1 To make the pasta, combine the flour, tarragon, and salt in a food processor. Beat together the egg, egg yolk, oil, and 2 tablespoons of the water. With the machine running, pour in the egg mixture and process until it forms a ball, leaving the sides of the bowl virtually clean. If the dough is crumbly, add the remaining water; if the dough is sticky, add 1–2 tablespoons flour and continue kneading in the food processor until a ball forms. Wrap

and chill for at least 30 minutes. Reserve the egg white.

2 To make the filling, put the chicken, lemon rind, and mixed herbs in a food processor and season with salt and pepper. Chop finely by pulsing; do not overprocess. Scrape into a bowl and stir in the cream. Taste and adjust the seasoning, if necessary.

3 Divide the pasta dough in half. Cover one half and roll the other half on a floured surface as thinly as possible, less than ¹⁄₁₆ inch. Cut out rectangles about 4 x 2 inches.

4 Place rounded teaspoons of filling on one half of the dough pieces. Brush around the edges with egg white and fold in half. Press the edges gently but

firmly to seal. Arrange the ravioli in one layer on a baking sheet, dusted generously with flour. Repeat with the remaining dough. Allow the ravioli to dry in a cool place for about 15 minutes or chill for 1–2 hours.

5 Bring a large quantity of salted water to a boil. Drop in half the ravioli and cook for 12–15 minutes until just tender. Drain on a clean dishtowel while cooking the remainder.

6 Meanwhile, put the stock and tarragon in a large saucepan. Bring to a boil and reduce the heat to bubble very gently. Cover and simmer for about 15 minutes, to infuse. Add the cooked ravioli to the stock and simmer for about 5 minutes until reheated. Ladle into warm soup plates to serve.

Pheasant Soup with Cider & Cream

*This an excellent soup to serve during the autumn,
when pheasant are widely available.*

Serves 6

INGREDIENTS

2 tbsp. butter

3 shallots, finely chopped

2 garlic cloves, thinly sliced

1¼ cups hard cider

5 cups pheasant or chicken stock

1 carrot, finely chopped

1 stalk celery, finely chopped

1 bay leaf

1 pheasant

10½ oz. potatoes, diced

9 oz. small button mushrooms, halved
   or quartered

1 large apple, peeled and diced

1¼ cups heavy cream

4 tbsp. cornstarch, diluted with 3
   tbsp. cold water

salt and pepper

TO GARNISH:

2 tbsp. olive oil, or as needed

30 sage leaves

1 Melt half of the butter in a large saucepan over a medium heat. Add the shallots and garlic and cook for 3–4 minutes, stirring frequently, until softened. Pour over the cider and bring to a boil. Add the stock, carrot, celery, bay leaf, and pheasant, which should be submerged. Bring back to a boil, reduce the heat, cover and simmer for about 1 hour, or until the pheasant is very tender. (Older pheasant may take longer.)

2 When the pheasant is cool enough to handle, remove the meat from the bones and cut into bite-sized pieces, discarding any fat. Strain the stock, pressing with the back of a spoon to extract all the liquid. Discard the vegetables and bay leaf. Remove as much fat as possible from the stock.

3 Put the pheasant stock in a large saucepan and bring to a boil. Adjust the heat so the liquid boils very gently. Add the potatoes and cook for about 15 minutes until they are just barely tender.

4 Meanwhile, melt the remaining butter in a large frying pan over a medium heat. Add the mushrooms and season with salt and pepper. Cook for 5–8 minutes until they are golden

brown, stirring on occasion, then more often once they start to change color.

5 Add the mushrooms to the soup, together with the apple and cream, and cook for about 10 minutes until the apple and potatoes are tender. Whisk the diluted cornstarch into the soup. Boil gently for 2–3 minutes, whisking, until slightly thickened. Then, add the pheasant meat and simmer gently until the soup is hot.

6 Heat the oil in a small frying pan until it starts to smoke. Add the sage leaves and fry for about 20 seconds until crispy. Drain on paper towels. Ladle the soup into warm bowls and garnish with crumbled fried sage.

Preserved Duck, Cabbage & Bean Soup

If you can't find the preserved duck confit that is traditionally used for this dish, you could braise duck legs in stock or substitute smoked chicken, but it will be a different soup.

Serves 6

INGREDIENTS

2 preserved duck legs
1 tbsp. duck fat or olive oil
1 onion, finely chopped
4 garlic cloves, finely chopped
2 carrots, sliced
1 large leek, halved lengthwise
  and sliced
2 turnips, diced

7 oz. dark leafy cabbage, such as
  cavolo nero or Savoy
5 cups chicken or duck stock
2 potatoes, diced
8 oz. dried white beans, soaked and
  cooked, or 14 oz. cans white beans
1 bay leaf
2 tbsp. roughly chopped fresh parsley

12 slices baguette
5½ oz. grated Gruyére cheese
salt and pepper

1 Scrape as much fat as possible from the preserved duck. Remove the duck meat from the bones, keeping it in large pieces; discard the skin and bones.

2 Heat the duck fat or oil in a large soup kettle or flameproof casserole over a medium heat. Add the onion and three-quarters of the garlic. Cover and cook for

3–4 minutes until just softened. Add the carrots, leek and turnips, cover and continue cooking for 20 minutes, stirring occasionally. If the vegetables start to brown, add a tablespoon of water.

3 Meanwhile, bring a large saucepan of salted water to a boil. Drop in the cabbage and boil gently for 5 minutes. Drain well.

4 Add the stock to the stewed vegetables. Stir in the potatoes, beans, parboiled cabbage and bay leaf, adjust seasoning. Bring almost to a boil, reduce the heat and simmer for 15 minutes.

5 Chop together the parsley and remaining garlic. Stir into the soup with the preserved duck, cover again and simmer for about 20 minutes, stirring occasionally. Season to taste.

6 Toast the bread under a preheated hot broiler on one side. Turn and top with the cheese. Broil until the cheese melts. Ladle the soup into warm bowls and top with the cheese toasts.

Parmesan Cheese Pancakes in Broth

This delicious soup has a rich homemade Italian-style meat stock as a base. A perfect dinner party starter, it is very light—and easy to make if you have a supply of the stock in the freezer.

Serves 4–6

INGREDIENTS

1 tbsp. all-purpose flour

2 tbsp. milk

2 eggs

2 tbsp. chopped fresh basil

3 tbsp. freshly grated Parmesan cheese, plus extra to serve

MEAT STOCK:

1 lb. chicken wings and/or legs

9 oz. lean boneless stewing beef, such as shin

6 cups water

1 celery stalk, thinly sliced

1 carrot, thinly sliced

1 onion, halved and sliced

2 garlic cloves, crushed

3–4 parsley stems

1 bay leaf

½ tsp. salt

pepper

1 To make the stock, put the chicken and beef in a large pot with the water, celery, carrot, onion, garlic, parsley stems, bay leaf, and salt. Bring just to a boil and skim off the foam that rises to the surface. Reduce the heat and simmer very gently, uncovered, for 2 hours.

2 Strain the stock and remove as much fat as possible. Discard the vegetables and herbs. Save the meat for another purpose.

3 Bring the stock to a boil in a clean saucepan. If necessary, boil to reduce the stock to 4 cups. Taste and adjust the seasoning (be restrained with salt). Reduce the heat and simmer gently while making the pancakes.

4 To make the pancakes, put the flour in a bowl and add half the milk. Whisk until smooth, add the remaining milk and whisk again. Break in the eggs and whisk to combine well. Season with salt

and pepper and stir in the basil and Parmesan.

5 Film the bottom of a small nonstick 6–7 inch frying pan with oil and heat until it begins to smoke. Pour in one-third of the batter (about 4 tablespoons) and tilt the pan so the batter covers the bottom. Cook for about 1 minute until mostly set around the edges. Turn the pancake and cook the other side for about 15 seconds. Turn out on to a plate. Continue making the remaining pancakes, adding more oil to the pan if needed.

6 Roll the pancakes up while warm, then cut into ⅛ inch slices across the roll to make spirals. Divide the pancake spirals among bowls. Ladle over the hot broth and serve with Parmesan.

French Onion Soup

A rich, flavorful homemade stock is the key to this satisfying soup.
While beef stock is traditional, a rich, intense chicken stock would be delicious as well.

Serves 6

INGREDIENTS

1 tbsp. butter

2 tbsp. olive oil

2 lb. 4 oz. large yellow onions, halved
  and sliced into half-circles

3 large garlic cloves, finely chopped

2 tbsp. all-purpose flour

¾ cup dry white wine

8 cups beef stock

3 tbsp. Cognac or brandy

6 slices French bread

7 oz. Gruyére cheese, grated

salt and pepper

1 Melt the butter with the oil in a large heavy-based saucepan over a medium heat. Add the onions and cook, covered, for 10–12 minutes until they soften, stirring occasionally. Add the garlic and sprinkle with salt and pepper.

2 Reduce the heat a little and continue cooking, uncovered, for 30–35 minutes, or until the onions turn a deep, golden brown, stirring from time to time until they start to color, then stirring more frequently and scraping the bottom of the pan as they begin to stick (see Cook's Tip).

3 Sprinkle over the flour and stir to blend. Stir in the white wine and bubble for 1 minute. Pour in the stock and bring to a boil, scraping the bottom of the pan and stirring to combine well. Reduce the heat to low, add the Cognac or brandy and simmer gently, stirring occasionally, for 45 minutes.

4 Toast the bread under a preheated hot broiler on one side. Turn over and top with the cheese, dividing it evenly. Broil until the cheese melts.

5 Place a piece of cheese toast in each of the 6 warmed bowls, then ladle the hot soup over. Serve at once.

COOK'S TIP

Don't try to hurry this soup. The rich flavor comes from cooking the onions slowly so their natural sugar caramelizes, then brewing them with the stock.

Roasted Corn Soup with Chilies

This soup is rich and exotic but relatively simple to make. Ancho chilies have a distinct smoky flavor, but if you can't find them, use chili paste instead.

Serves 4

INGREDIENTS

1 dried ancho chili
4 tbsp. butter
1 lb. 2 oz. defrosted frozen sweetcorn
   kernels
1 large onion, finely chopped
1 large garlic clove, finely chopped

1 red bell pepper, cored, deseeded and
   finely chopped
1¼ cups chicken stock or water
2½ cups whipping cream
½ tsp. ground cumin
salt

chopped fresh cilantro or parsley, to
   garnish

1 Put the chili in a bowl and cover with boiling water. Stand about 15 minutes to soften.

2 Melt the butter in a frying pan over a medium-low heat. Add the sweetcorn and turn to coat. Cook for about 15 minutes, stirring frequently, until it starts to brown slightly. Add the onion, garlic and bell pepper and cook for about 7–10 minutes, stirring frequently, until the onion is softened and the mixture starts to stick.

3 Transfer the mixture to a blender or food processor, add the stock and purée until smooth.

4 Put the cream in a large saucepan, stir in the puréed vegetables and bring almost to a boil. Add the cumin. Season with a little salt. Adjust the heat so the soup bubbles very gently and cook until the mixture is reduced by about one-quarter.

5 Remove the ancho chili from its liquid and discard the core and the seeds. (Wash hands well after touching chilies.) Put the chili into a blender or food processor with 4–5 tablespoons of the soaking water and purée until smooth. Stir 2–4 tablespoons of the purée into the soup, according to taste, and continue cooking for an additional 5 minutes.

6 Taste the soup and adjust the seasoning, if necessary. Ladle the soup into warm bowls, garnish with cilantro or parsley and serve.

Melon Gazpacho

*Glass bowls are pretty for serving this soup,
which makes a very light starter for warm days.*

Serves 4

INGREDIENTS

1 tsp. oil
1 onion, finely chopped
1 large garlic clove, finely chopped
1 tsp. chopped fresh chili

1 lb. 9 oz. seedless cantaloupe melon
   flesh, cubed
½ tsp. raspberry vinegar, or 1 tsp.
   lemon juice

pinch of salt
½ ripe green melon, such as
   Honeydew (about 1 lb. 2 oz)
snipped chives, to garnish

1 Heat the oil in a small pan over a low heat. Add the onion, garlic and chili, cover and cook for 6–7 minutes, stirring occasionally, until the onion is soft but not browned.

2 Put the cantaloupe melon flesh in a blender or food processor, add the onion, garlic, and chili and purée until smooth, stopping to scrape down the sides as needed. (You may need to work in batches.) Add the vinegar or lemon juice with the salt and process to combine.

3 Chill for about 30 minutes, or until the mixture is cold.

4 Remove the seeds from the green melon, then cut into balls with a melon baller. Or alternatively, cut into cubes with a sharp knife.

5 Divide the soup among 4 shallow bowls and top with the green melon balls. Sprinkle lightly with chives to garnish and serve.

COOK'S TIP

If you are wary of using fresh chili, omit it and add a few drops of store-bought hot sauce to taste, at the end of Step 2, to liven up the soup.

VARIATION

Substitute watermelon for the cantaloupe and use contrasting melon balls for serving.

Cold Tomato, Carrot, & Orange Soup

This soup is made from raw vegetables and fruit, so it is full of goodness as well as good taste and is wonderfully refreshing on a warm day.

Serves 4

INGREDIENTS

3 large seedless oranges
4 ripe tomatoes
2 stalks celery, strings removed,
   chopped

3 carrots, grated
1½ cups tomato juice
salt
Tabasco sauce (optional)

1 tbsp. chopped fresh mint
fresh mint sprigs, to garnish

1 Working over a bowl to catch the juices, peel the oranges. Cut down between the membranes and drop the orange segments into the bowl.

2 Put the tomatoes in a small bowl and pour over boiling water to cover. Allow to stand for 10 seconds, then drain. Peel off the skin and cut the tomatoes in half crossways. Scoop out the seeds into a sieve set over a bowl; reserve the tomato juices.

3 Put the tomatoes, celery, and carrots in a blender (or food processor). Add the orange segments and their juice and the juice saved from the tomatoes. Purée until smooth.

4 Scrape into a bowl and stir in the tomato juice. Cover and chill until cold.

5 Taste the soup and add salt, if needed, and a few drops of Tabasco sauce to heighten the flavor, if desired. Stir in the chopped mint, ladle into cold bowls and garnish with fresh mint sprigs.

COOK'S TIP

This soup really needs to be made in a blender for the best texture. A food processor can be used but the soup will not be completely smooth.

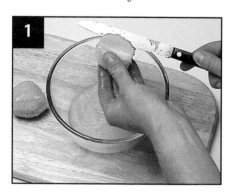

Chilled Avocado & Almond Soup

This rich-tasting cold soup has an inviting color and would make an appetizing start to a dinner party.

Serves 4

INGREDIENTS

2½ cups water
1 onion, finely chopped
1 stalk celery, finely chopped
1 carrot, grated
4 garlic cloves, chopped or crushed

1 bay leaf
½ tsp. salt
¾ cup ground almonds
2 ripe avocados (about 1 lb.)
3–4 tbsp. fresh lemon juice

salt
snipped chives, to garnish

1 Combine the water, onion, celery, carrot, garlic, and bay leaf in a saucepan with the salt. Bring to a boil, reduce the heat, cover and simmer for about 30 minutes, or until the vegetables are very tender.

2 Strain the soup base, reserving the liquid and vegetables separately.

3 Put the vegetables into a blender or food processor.

Add the almonds and a small amount of the liquid and purée until very smooth, scraping down the sides as necessary. Add as much of the remaining liquid as the capacity of the blender or processor permits and process to combine. Scrape into a bowl, stir in any remaining liquid and chill until cold.

4 Cut the avocados in half, discard the stones and scoop the flesh into the blender or food

processor. Add the cold soup base and purée until smooth, scraping down the sides as necessary. For a thinner consistency, add a few spoonfuls of cold water.

5 Add the lemon juice and season with salt to taste. Ladle into chilled small bowls and sprinkle each serving lightly with chives.

Watercress Vichyssoise

Traditional vichyssoise is simply cold leek and potato soup flavored with chives.
The addition of watercress gives it a refreshing flavor and lovely cool color.

Serves 6

INGREDIENTS

1 tbsp. olive oil

3 large leeks, thinly sliced (about 12 oz.)

1 large potato, finely diced (about 12 oz.)

2½ cups chicken or vegetable stock

2 cups water

1 bay leaf

6 oz. prepared watercress

¾ cup light cream

salt and pepper

watercress leaves, to garnish

1 Heat the oil in a heavy-based saucepan over a medium heat. Add the leeks and cook for about 3 minutes, stirring frequently, until they begin to soften.

2 Add the potato, stock, water, and bay leaf. Add salt if the stock is unsalted. Bring to a boil, reduce the heat, cover and cook gently for about 25 minutes until the vegetables are tender. It may be difficult to find the bay leaf, however it is best removed.

3 Add the watercress and continue to cook for an additional 2–3 minutes, stirring frequently, just until the watercress is completely wilted.

4 Allow the soup to cool slightly, then transfer to a blender or food processor and purée until smooth, working in batches if necessary. (If using a food processor, strain off the cooking liquid and reserve. Purée the soup solids with enough cooking liquid to moisten them, then combine with the remaining liquid.)

5 Put the soup in a large bowl and stir in half the cream. Season with salt, if needed, and plenty of pepper.

6 Refrigerate until cold. Taste and adjust the seasoning, if necessary. Ladle into chilled bowls, drizzle the remaining cream on top and garnish with watercress leaves. Serve at once.

Chilled Borscht

There are innumerable versions of this soup of Eastern European origin.
This refreshing vegetarian version is light and flavorful.

Serves 4–6

INGREDIENTS

¼ medium cabbage, cored and
   coarsely chopped
1 tbsp. vegetable oil
1 onion, finely chopped
1 leek, halved lengthwise and sliced
14 oz. can peeled tomatoes in juice
5 cups water, plus extra if needed

1 carrot, thinly sliced
1 small parsnip, finely chopped
3 beet (raw or cooked), peeled and
   cubed
1 bay leaf
1½ cups tomato juice
2–3 tbsp. chopped fresh dill

fresh lemon juice (optional)
salt and pepper
sour cream or yogurt, to garnish

1 Cover the cabbage generously with cold water in a pan. Bring to a boil, boil for 3 minutes, then drain.

2 Heat the oil in a large saucepan over a medium-low heat. Add the onion and leek, cover and cook for about 5 minutes, stirring occasionally, until the vegetables begin to soften.

3 Add the tomatoes, water, carrot, parsnip, beet, and bay

leaf. Stir in the blanched cabbage and add a large pinch of salt. Bring to a boil, reduce the heat and simmer for about 1¼ hours until all the vegetables are tender. Remove the bay leaf, if possible.

4 Allow the soup to cool slightly, then transfer to a blender or food processor and purée until smooth, working in batches if necessary. (If using a food processor, strain off the cooking liquid and reserve. Purée

the soup solids with enough cooking liquid to moisten them, then combine with the remaining liquid.)

5 Scrape the soup into a large container and stir in the tomato juice. Allow to cool and refrigerate until cold.

6 Add the dill and stir. Thin the soup with more tomato juice or water, if desired. Season to taste with salt and pepper and, if you prefer it less sweet, add a few drops of lemon juice. Ladle into chilled soup bowls, top each with a spiral of sour cream or a dollop of yogurt.

Iced Salsa Soup

A chunky mix of colorful vegetables, highlighted with Mexican flavors, this cold soup makes a lively starter to any meal.

Serves 4

INGREDIENTS

2 large ears of corn, or 8 oz. frozen sweetcorn kernels

1 tbsp. olive oil

1 orange or red bell pepper, cored, deseeded and finely chopped

1 green bell pepper, cored, deseeded and finely chopped

1 sweet onion, such as Vidalia, finely chopped

3 ripe tomatoes, skinned, deseeded and chopped

½ tsp. chili powder, or to taste

½ cup water

2 cups tomato juice

chili paste (optional)

salt and pepper

TO GARNISH:

3–4 scallions, finely chopped

cilantro

1 Cut the corn kernels from the cobs, or if using frozen corn, defrost, and drain.

2 Heat the oil in a saucepan over a medium-high heat. Add the bell peppers and cook, stirring briskly, for 3 minutes. Add the onion and continue cooking for about 2 minutes, or until it starts to color slightly.

3 Add the tomatoes, corn, and chili powder. Continue cooking, stirring frequently, for 1 minute. Pour in the water and when it bubbles, reduce the heat, cover and cook for an additional 4–5 minutes, or until the bell peppers are just barely tender.

4 Transfer the mixture to a large container and stir in the tomato juice. Season with salt and

pepper and add more chili powder if desired. Cover and refrigerate until cold.

5 Taste and adjust the seasoning. For a more spicy soup, stir in a little chili paste to taste. For a thinner soup, add a small amount of iced water. Ladle into chilled bowls and garnish with scallion and cilantro.

Cold Cucumber
& Smoked Salmon Soup

When cucumber is cooked it becomes a much more subtle vegetable,
perfect to set off the taste of smoked salmon. This cold soup makes a lovely starter.

Serves 4

INGREDIENTS

2 tsp. oil
1 large onion, finely chopped
1 large cucumber, peeled, deseeded
  and sliced
1 small potato, diced

1 stalk celery, finely chopped
4 cups chicken or vegetable stock
1²/₃ cup heavy cream
5½ oz. smoked salmon, finely diced
2 tbsp. chopped fresh chives

salt and pepper
fresh dill sprigs, to garnish

1 Heat the oil in a large sauce-pan over a medium heat. Add the onion and cook for about 3 minutes until it begins to soften.

2 Add the cucumber, potato, celery, and stock, along with a large pinch of salt, if using unsalted stock. Bring to a boil, reduce the heat, cover and cook gently for about 20 minutes until the vegetables are tender.

3 Allow the soup to cool slightly, then transfer to a blender or food processor, working in batches if necessary.

4 Purée the soup until smooth. If using a food processor, strain off the cooking liquid and reserve it. Purée the soup solids with enough cooking liquid to moisten them, then combine with the remaining liquid.

5 Transfer the puréed soup into a large container. Cover and refrigerate until cold.

6 Stir the cream, salmon, and chives into the soup. If time permits, chill for at least 1 hour to allow the flavors to blend. Taste and adjust the seasoning, adding salt, if needed, and pepper. Ladle into chilled bowls and garnish with dill.

Spicy Red Pepper Soup

This brilliantly colored soup makes a great summer starter,
especially when bell peppers are abundant in farm markets—or in your garden.

Serves 6

INGREDIENTS

1 tbsp. olive oil
1 lb. leeks, thinly sliced
1 large onion, halved and thinly sliced
2 garlic cloves, finely chopped or
  crushed

6 red bell peppers, cored, deseeded
  and sliced
4 cups water
½ tsp. ground cumin
½ tsp. ground coriander

1 tsp. chili paste, or to taste
1–2 tsp. fresh lemon juice
salt and pepper
finely chopped spring onion (scallion)
  greens or chives, to garnish

1 Heat the oil in a large saucepan over a medium heat. Add the leeks, onion and garlic and cook, covered, for about 5 minutes until the onion is softened, stirring frequently.

2 Stir in the bell peppers and cook for an additional 2–3 minutes. Add the water, cumin, ground coriander, and chili paste together with a large pinch of salt. Bring to a boil, reduce the heat, cover and simmer for about 35 minutes until all the vegetables are tender.

3 Allow the soup to cool slightly, then transfer to a blender or food processor and purée until smooth, working in batches if necessary. (If using a food processor, strain off the cooking liquid and reserve. Purée the soup solids with enough cooking liquid to moisten them, then combine with the remaining liquid.)

4 Put the soup in a large bowl, then season with salt and pepper and add lemon juice, to taste. Allow to cool completely, cover and chill in the refrigerator until cold.

5 Before serving, taste and adjust the seasoning, if necessary. Add a little more chili paste if a spicy taste is preferred. Ladle into chilled bowls and garnish with scallion greens or chives.

Melon & Ginger Soup

Almost any variety of melon is appropriate, including honeydew, galia, watermelon, Crenshaw, charentais, or cantaloupe, but it is essential that the melon be ripe.

Serves 4

INGREDIENTS

1 large ripe melon (about 2 lb. 4 oz)
¾ tsp. grated peeled fresh ginger
　root, or more
1 tbsp. fresh lemon juice, or to taste

1 tsp. sugar
½ cup whipping cream
salt
snipped fresh chives, to garnish

1 Halve the melon, discard the seeds and scoop the flesh into a blender or food processor. Purée until smooth, stopping to scrape down the sides as necessary. (You may need to work in batches.)

2 Add the grated ginger, lemon juice, and sugar with a pinch of salt and process to combine. Taste and add a little more ginger, if desired. Scrape into a bowl, cover and chill completely, usually for about 30 minutes, or until cold.

3 Add the cream and stir to combine well. Taste and adjust the seasoning, adding a little more salt and lemon juice if necessary.

4 To serve, divide the melon purée among four chilled bowls and garnish with chives.

COOK'S TIP

To determine the ripeness of melon, gently press the end opposite the stem—it should give a little, and there is usually a characteristic aroma on pressing that helps to confirm the verdict.

VARIATION

If you prefer, use strained yogurt instead of cream.

Cucumber Soup with Walnuts & Yogurt

Parsley tames the pungent garlic flavor of this traditional Balkan soup.
The cucumber and yogurt make it a refreshing summer starter.

Serves 4

INGREDIENTS

1 large cucumber
½ cup walnut pieces, toasted (see Cook's Tip)
½ cup parsley, leaves only
1 small garlic clove, very finely

chopped
2 tbsp. olive oil
4 tbsp. water
1 tbsp. fresh lemon juice, or to taste
1¼ cups strained yogurt

salt and pepper
fresh mint leaves, to garnish

1 Peel the cucumber, slice lengthwise and scoop out the seeds with a small sharp spoon. Cut the flesh into 1 inch pieces.

2 Put the walnuts, parsley leaves, garlic, oil, and water in a blender or food processor with half of the cucumber and purée until smooth, stopping to scrape down the sides as necessary.

3 Add the remaining cucumber to the blender or processor with a pinch of salt and the lemon juice. Purée until smooth.

4 Scrape the purée into a large bowl and stir in the yogurt. Season to taste with salt and pepper and add a little more lemon juice, if desired.

5 Cover and chill for about 30 minutes, or until cold. Taste and adjust the seasoning, if necessary. Ladle into chilled bowls and garnish with mint leaves.

COOK'S TIP

Toasting the walnuts gives them extra flavor. Just heat them in a dry frying pan over a medium-low heat until they begin to color and smell aromatic.

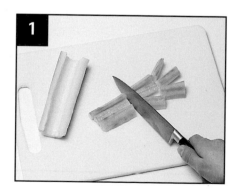

Cold Fresh Cilantro Soup

This soup brings together Thai flavors for a cool refreshing starter.
It highlights fresh cilantro, now much more widely available.

Serves 4

INGREDIENTS

2 tsp. olive oil
1 large onion, finely chopped
1 leek, thinly sliced
1 garlic clove, thinly sliced
4 cups water

1 zucchini, about 7 oz., peeled and
  chopped
4 tbsp. white rice
2 inch piece lemon grass
2 lime leaves

½ cup cilantro and soft stems
chili paste, (optional)
salt and pepper
finely chopped red bell pepper and/or
  red chilies, to garnish

1 Heat the oil in a large saucepan over a medium heat. Add the onion, leek, and garlic, cover and cook for 4–5 minutes until the onion is softened, stirring frequently.

2 Add the water, zucchini and rice with a large pinch of salt and some pepper. Stir in the lemon grass and lime leaves. Bring just to a boil and reduce the heat to low. Cover and simmer for about 15–20 minutes until the rice is soft and tender.

3 Add the cilantro, pushing them down into the liquid. Continue cooking for 2–3 minutes until they are wilted. Remove the lemon grass and lime leaves.

4 Allow the soup to cool slightly, then transfer to a blender or food processor and purée until smooth, working in batches if necessary. (If using a food processor, strain off the cooking liquid and reserve for later. Purée the soup solids with enough cooking liquid to moisten them, then combine with the remaining liquid.)

5 Scrape the soup into a large container. Season to taste with salt and pepper. Cover and refrigerate until cold.

6 Taste and adjust the seasoning. For a more spicy soup, stir in a little chili paste to taste. For a thinner soup, add a small amount of iced water. Ladle into chilled bowls and garnish with finely chopped red bell pepper and/or chilies.

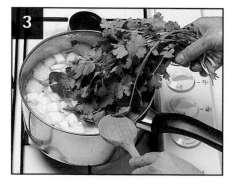

Index